THE STAINED GLASS HOUSE

A Handbook for Ministers' Wives

by
Yvonne Garrett

Vernon House
Houston, Texas

All Scripture quotations, unless otherwise noted, are from the King James
Version of the Bible. The quotations marked NEB are from *The New English
Bible*, © The Delegates of The Oxford University Press and The Syndics of
The Cambridge University Press 1961, 1970.

Published by Vernon House, 7480 Beechnut, #507, Houston, TX 77074

Manufactured by Gulf Publishing Company, Houston, TX

Cover design by Pat Hardesty

Library of Congress Catalog Card No.: 91–74060

ISBN 0–88415–044–5

Printed in the United States of America

Contents

Introduction

More than two hundred ministers' wives helped me write this book. They filled out questionnaires and shared feelings, frustrations and suggestions. Then there were those who wrote books and articles that fit right in. I talked with sons and daughters of ministers. Church members from several congregations answered a telephone survey to produce a Profile of the Ideal Minister's Wife. In many cities I sat in on seminars, classes and meetings attended by ministers' wives. (See page 6 for a copy of the questionnaire used in my survey.)

Of course, I started with tremendous resources right in my own family. I am married to the son of a preacher. From him I have seen first-hand the long-term Christian attributes one acquires while growing up in a minister's family. Along with my preacher father-in-law, I have a sister-in-law and two nieces who are wives of ministers and a son-in-law who is the son of a minister. These people you will meet in the book.

(Conversations and incidents are from real experiences, but often, in deference to privacy, I have used composites of people and changed names and settings.)

I grew up in a family active in the work of the church. Preacher-and-fried-chicken was common Sunday fare at our house. From early childhood I have observed, scrutinized, respected, appreciated, adored and prayed for ministers' wives. Writing this book has been my serendipity.

Questionnaire

Age group: 20-30 ( )   30-40 ( )   40-50 ( )   above 50 ( )

1. Do you consider yourself "called" to be a minister's wife?
2. Do you and your husband pray together? How much spiritual growth time do you spend together per week?
3. To whom do you (or would you) go for emotional and/or spiritual help?
4. To whom does (or would) your husband go for emotional and/or spiritual help?
5. Do you work outside the home?
6. If you do work outside the home, why?
7. If you do not work outside the home, why not?
8. Do you feel that your closest friend or friends should be members of your husband's congregation?
9. Do you feel that your husband's estimate of women is heightened or lowered by his contact with the women members of your church? In what way?
10. Do you feel that intimacy between you and your husband is affected by his association with the female members of your church?
11. Is (or was) your father a minister?
12. Is (or was) your father-in-law a minister?
13. If your husband were not a minister, what career do you think he would have chosen?
14. Do you consider pastors' salaries generally adequate?
15. How would (or did) you handle the situation if your teen-age son or daughter decided not to attend services of the church?
16. Do you think your child's behavior affects your husband's effectiveness as a minister?
17. What do you like best about being a minister's wife?
18. What do you dislike most about being a minister's wife?

The Changing Role of the Minister's Wife

Janet Pierson didn't want to marry a preacher. She had prayed against it all her life: "Lord, please don't let me fall in love with a preacher." With her dad a school teacher and both her sisters married to lawyers, there was no way she was going to call home and say, "Hey, guess what, I'm going to marry a preacher." But when she fell in love, she changed her prayer: "Forget what I said, Lord; just make him love me."

On the day I talked with Janet, she laughed about her fickle petitions. "How God must have enjoyed all that! I didn't know Tom was a Religion major until I was smitten beyond recall. He didn't look like a Pre-Preach; he didn't wear a coat and tie or carry a Bible under his arm or embellish his conversation with Jesus jargon. He was so normal."

The *normal* guy we call a minister and the life he leads have long been an enigma to people in and out of the church. But not to his wife. I've asked many wives (including 120 who filled out questionnaires for me), "What do you like best about being a minister's wife?"—and the number one answer was "being married to my husband." Then I asked, "Knowing what you know now, would you, given a second chance, marry a minister?" Only twice did I get a negative answer; the others: "I would marry John, yes," or, "If the minister were Bob, I'd marry him." One wife, getting out her double message, replied, "Being a pastor's wife is a small price to pay for getting to be married to Charles."

Still, the minister's wife, by association, shares the enigma. When I was a child at my mother's knee, I heard her and her friends discuss a beautiful young girl of the community who refused to marry her handsome young beau because he was going to be a preacher. I couldn't understand that. My mother and her friends couldn't understand it either. Imagine a girl's not wanting to be a preacher's wife!

I still consider it an elevated position. Oh, I've brought it down to earth through the years and I've learned to relate to it. My closest friend in college married a preacher-medical-missionary. My life has been infused with wives, daughters and mothers of ministers ever since. All of which has kept my admiration intact. But I can understand Janet's initial aversion to a life of clergy, just as I can understand her current satisfaction. She had heard all the platitudes about demands made on preachers' families, lack of privacy, gossiping members, clinging women, the heartless elders. And she has encountered all of these, in varying degrees. But, as she would have you know, "Once I got the chip off my shoulder, I started becoming a really decent pastor's wife."

My niece Cathy Johnson began her married life supporting this same chip. A week before her wedding, she had the gloomy scene perfected: "No one is going to want David for a pastor because I won't be the *normal* preacher's wife." That word "normal" again. She explained the "normal preacher's wife" precept. "Well, I won't be teaching the children in Sunday School or going to the Missionary Society meetings or accompanying 'the pastor' on his calls. I'll have my own career and it will be full time. 'They' won't like that."

Cathy and a surprisingly large number of her sisters-of-the-cloth fall into this category. They would understand Jean Reynolds Davis when she wrote, "Woefully, I saw myself playing hymns at prayer meetings, dusting the tome-cluttered study, hovering over the tea table like a picky crow: a pale, impoverished pilgrim searching with hungry eyes for some bright fortune in the matted tea leaves."[1]

Janet can relate to all this. She too was braced for the onslaught. Which never came, really. Skirmishes, yes. And a few battles, mostly with her self.

What changed, Janet?

"*I* did. I looked around me and saw that other wives were enduring. Even more than that; they were thriving. And I observed that my friends—wives of teachers, doctors, businessmen—had situations much like mine."

Two things happened to give impetus to Janet's determination to be a good wife to Tom. First, during Tom's first full-time job, one as an associate pastor, Janet's best friend was a doctor's wife. While Tom was spending long hours in hospital visitation, counseling, studying, the young doctor was spending *days* away from home, completing his internship. His wife spent many evenings in the Pierson apartment, overcome with loneliness. This helped Janet get her role in perspective.

Then, Janet's second sister, married to the lawyer, was divorced. "That's when I knew it wasn't the profession that made the difference; it was the man."

Janet realizes that being a minister's wife these days isn't the same as it used to be, better in some ways, worse in others, it really doesn't matter. Each person has to function in her own time and space, according to her own ability and durability.

Martha Nelson said she knew the times had changed when she saw her church's Missionary Society director arrive at a meeting on a bike, in jeans, with a red scarf pulling back her pony tail, and her Bible and program materials in a knapsack on her back.[2]

If you had been with me recently as I stood in my father-in-law's library, I would have said to you, "See, this is evidence of how your role has changed." My father-in-law started preaching half a century ago and he has accumulated 782 books (we counted them!) and I could not find *one* about or for the minister's wife! Yet I have in my recently compiled collection numerous books on the subject.

So the role, like the times, has changed. Not just for ministers' wives, but for all wives. Janet and I discussed how women in other professions have contributed to this difference. For example, I've talked lately with three medical students who are attending classes with their husbands, a prevailing movement. It is common knowledge that women are setting the trend in public accounting. A recent statistic indicates that the number of female law students in our country is fast approaching 50 percent. In professions, in business, in politics, women are at the forefront. They have a choice. Most churches recognize this. No longer is it assumed that the pastor's wife plays the piano. (But one wife said she started taking piano lessons as soon as she and her husband became engaged—"just in case.") You may even take classes alongside your husband in seminary and go to work in churches as a team, much as was expected years ago when churches were accused of "getting two for the price of one." A bit of expertise in church education, ethics, even sermon preparation might take some of the fear out of the "whither thou goest" and also entice the church fathers on your behalf as they consider your husband.

Gina Ross recalled the day she went with her husband for his first interview with a church. On one lapel of her suit she wore a Sunday School attendance pin and on the other lapel her college choir pin. "I was really surprised that we didn't get that job; I thought that at least I had made a good impression."

There are twenty-three million dual-career marriages in the United States; the clergy certainly is not excluded from this list. In our survey of ministers' wives, 52 of the 120 work outside the home. The leading reason was for the additional paycheck, but many felt it gives them greater opportunities to use their talents and be of service. Therefore as we look at the minister's wife in this study, obviously it will be necessary to consider the wife who combines home-making with a second career.

Of course, many are not choosing that second career because of (1) children to raise, (2) the desire to be more available to their husbands, (3) a preference for strong church involvement and (4) the desire for a less structured lifestyle. In that order, these are the reasons listed in our survey for not working outside the home. One wife wrote, "I like keeping house, working in my garden, giving parties. I like not being exhausted at the end of the day and, best of all, I like being available to go with my husband—on short visits or long trips."

Yet ministers' wives themselves have blazed the trails for all the Janets and Cathys and Ginas of today; they are the ones who have created prerogatives, developed assertiveness and have loved their ways into the hearts of their people; yes, *loved* their people.

Gina said she was trying so hard to be the perfect pastor's wife that she was bogged down with commandments, trying to do all the right things. Then one afternoon at a day care center she saw a little girl with a short, twisted leg who couldn't run and play with the other children, who was "so pitiful I just wanted to take her in my arms and love her. I couldn't forget her. A few nights later when I couldn't sleep for thinking about her, it came to me that this is what I should be doing—loving people; then I wouldn't have to worry about what to do and what not to do."

There was a day, according to Deanna Harrison, when the minister's wife had to fit into a convenient mold. "It came in handy, since everyone knew what to expect from her, and she knew exactly what she was expected to do."[3]

I spent a delightful afternoon with Madie Merle Westmoreland, widow of a prominent Houston pastor. From time to time, she would look at my tape recorder and ask, "Is that on? Turn it off and I'll explain something to you." From what *is* on my recorder, I share wisdom. When we finished our conversation and she had brought out her laden tea tray, I asked her to summarize her views, to pass on advice to younger ministers' wives. I had expected three or four concise statements; I got ten:

1. Rely on the Lord.
2. Don't take another preacher's wife as your model; you might become disillusioned.
3. Have close friends; you'll need them.
4. Never give up on *any*one.
5. Never add fuel to the fire. (Don't even give the appearance of agreeing with tales told to you; someone may report that you *said* it.)
6. Make your home a sanctuary, especially for your husband.
7. Be sure your children know their father.
8. Be ye kind.
9. Remember that overcoming problems makes you stronger, and
10. Growing older brings wisdom.

She has blazed trails.

Then I had conversations over lunch and dinner and conference tables with a co-worker who is very young and just beginning her trail. Her husband is a student and pastor of a small rural church; most of the members are the ages of her grandparents. She is learning from them; somehow she is a jump ahead on the "loving" part. Making house calls with her husband on Saturdays is pure pleasure. "And sometimes on Sundays, my most important responsibility is to sit and hold the hand of someone whose husband died that week."

Assertiveness does not root out love. Janie Garrett, who is married to our nephew, is a person who knows her talents and continually comes up with ways to use them. She seems always to have found, or created, freedom to innovate-and-conform. "I like being a preacher's wife," she said, "and I accept my responsibilities as one. I find no contradiction in that statement and in saying to my church 'I choose not to work with children and teen-agers or music or education or on the social committee. I like adult missions; that's where I want to make my impact.'" Kay Warren said, "I can visit healthy people seven days a week, but hospitals I just can't handle. Yet. Someday I'm sure I'll graduate to that; in the meantime, I'm fulfilling a very needed role in our new church in a new area—knocking on doors and doing church PR."

In explaining her evolvement into church duties, Denise Turner said, "I had certainly not been required to demonstrate any musical talent when I applied for a license to marry a minister. I didn't even have to pray out loud in front of the county clerk. Later, of course, I did hear that piano-playing could be a real plus; and I promptly brushed up on my scales....I soon knew that I had only two choices left. I could either play loudly and pretend not to hear the E sharps, or I could carve out my own special niche in the church."[4]

In most churches, you won't be expected to fit the mold of the previous pastor's wife or anyone else. And if you don't like being called "the preacher's wife," let them know. (I was surprised at the volatile response this title provokes in so many wives.) If you want to teach a Bible class or don't want to teach a Bible class, your wishes likely will be honored (at least, by most members). If you have special wishes for privacy, home life, pursuit of hobbies or projects (we'll deal with this in other chapters), the average congregation will respect them. A study from a North Carolina ministry commission reports: "There is no clear pattern of role for the wives of ministers. Each wife, with her husband and congregation, is forced to clarify her own sense of identity."[5]

At a youth encampment, the girls' dress code prohibited short shorts, but the Youth Minister's wife wore short shorts and halters while her husband's young charges wore shirts and walking shorts. Another minister's wife hit town by announcing to all who would listen that she planned to join a tennis club, play tennis and bridge and "do all the things I couldn't do at the church we just left."

This isn't exactly what the North Carolina commission meant by clarifying one's sense of identity; such tactics are more muddling than clarifying. It's hard to find the real woman behind such flaunting. Beauty and joy must "reside in the inmost center of your being," we are told: "a gentle, quiet spirit, which is of high value in the sight of the Lord" (1 Pet. 3:3-4).

Being someone other than yourself is hardly worth the effort. Deception eventually wears you down. Like Denise Turner, find your own niche in church and in life; you'll be more comfortable, to say the least.

When I was a new accountant's wife, I was awed by the talents of the other wives with whom I spent a great deal of time. I knew I could never measure up to their poise and charm, but I was accepted for myself and it was unnecessary to even consider trying to be like someone else.

Someone has said it is the group in the middle, age-wise, that is making most of the adjustments; a Mrs. Westmoreland at one end of the scale, a Cathy or a Janie at the other. Sounds plausible. The theory is that for younger ones, the changes have been perfected; for the older ones, the changes came *after* their tenure. So the middle group inherits the positives, and negatives, of both worlds, a blending of challenges and guidelines.

In my interviews when I asked, "What advice would you give to a person who is just beginning her life as a minister's wife?," almost everyone answered, "Be yourself." I know what they mean, though I think often it is a stock answer. And I know many wives who are not sure of how to be themselves or if they like what "yourself" really is. I was in that situation on one memorable occasion. I was going along fine being the mother of five children, three of them in elementary school, when one day I read an article that said a good mother greets her children at the end of a school day clean, cheerful and relaxed. She sits down with them over milk and cookies and discusses the events of the day. So I determined from that day forward to be just such a mother! I rushed through my chores, brushed my hair, got out the Oreos and waited for the school bus. A few weeks later, in honor of Mother's Day, the children in my son's third grade room wrote papers on "My Mother." My son Doug wrote, "My mother goes to parties. My mother takes naps. My mother likes cookies..." So, I went back to my role of the harried mother with mop in hand.

By trial and error you will learn not only how to be yourself, but you will learn other rewarding lessons. Janie learned to forgive people. She hadn't planned to; she felt she had "every right" to be angry at these members. When I asked her how it feels to forgive someone, she said, "Oh, it's such fun." One wife *knew* she could "win over" the family who objected to her husband's idea of adding a new staff member, even though her husband had given up. She had confidence in her "self." It took a long time, but she, with her unofficial committee, did it. "Never give up on anyone," said Mrs. Westmoreland. Be yourself, but be bendable.

When Hurricane Carla hit Houston, we stood at our kitchen window and watched the pine trees in our back yard bend all the way to the ground, then up again, over and over and over, with never a crack or blemish. We said we knew then the truth of the description "the sturdy pine." So it is with people. Being pliable is evidence of stability.

The role has changed. Maybe you're not the "elect lady" you would have been fifty years ago or the foreteller-of-new-ideas of twenty-five years ago, but your field is bigger; you have more freedom to try your wings, to fall or fly.

Nothing is new, really. My sons, who during their college years had elephant-eye-high stacks of record albums and could discuss with authority the contributing musicians, were surprised to learn that the Rolling Stones are not new, that the title was used first in the book of Joshua. And certainly human nature is not new. Even though your role has gone through the usual process of transformation, you still are involved with *people*, just as were Mrs. Westmoreland and all the generations of ministers' wives that went before her.

My father was an itinerant farmer, and one of the first things he would do when he started working a piece of land was to plant an orchard. However, he seldom lived in one place long enough to see the trees produce fruit. It may be the same with you. In some churches you won't be able to do all the things you'd like to do or do them the way you'd like to do them. Yet those who come after you will benefit from the seeds you plant.

NOTES

1. Jean Reynolds Davis, *A Hat on the Hall Table* (New York: Harper and Row, 1967), p. 2.
2. Martha Nelson, *This Call We Share* (Nashville: Broadman, 1977), p. 22.
3. Deanna Harrison, "Secrets of A Minister's Wife," *Baptist Standard*, Dec. 2, 1981, p. 11.
4. Denise Turner, *Home Sweet Fishbowl* (Waco, TX: Word Books, 1982), p. 21.
5. *Commission on Ministry Report*, Baptist State Convention of North Carolina, Nov. 1981, p. 20.

Finding Your Place in the Church

Our son Richard was explaining the exhilaration of running cross-country with his high school track team: "At first, when I'm getting my pace, I ask myself, 'What on earth am I doing here?' Then, later, I feel I could run forever."

In most churches, you probably will start the same way, except you'll *know* why you're there—because your husband is. But some of the jobs you undertake, some of the situations you find yourself in, may make you doubt your sanity, and your husband's. Eventually, however, if the reports I get are true, you will feel you could "run forever."

Before you launch into the great, vast unknown, do your homework. Often when my husband and I take a trip, I do well to get my suitcase packed and leave phone numbers on the refrigerator; I don't have time to go by Triple-A for literature or get out the *National Geographic* and read. But I always wish I had. It's fun to know about places as you travel along as well as to read about them on your return. So before you go to a new church or a new community, get all available information: church organization, contributions of the church to the town and the town to the church, the people you'll be working and living with and their expectations of you.

My friend Helen said that her experience as a preacher's wife taught her that there are two basic needs for every minister's wife, especially those new to the field: (1) have a knowledge of expectations, and (2) be a committed Christian, but not necessarily in that order.

One pastor was explaining why a valuable staff member had resigned. "To some extent, it's our fault; we neglected to explain that our staff wives are almost as busy here as their husbands are. She felt unable to keep up." Janet Pierson told of a friend who moved into a new church assuming she'd be welcomed with open arms in the children's area because of her expertise, but found that the only way she could be used was to push someone else out. So, as second choice, she went to work in the Youth area. Several months later, when a pre-school director was needed, she was so ensconced with her high-schoolers that she wouldn't have dreamed of leaving them. All disappointments are not so easily resolved, so it helps to know what you're walking into or not walking into.

Of course, the size of the church makes a great deal of difference. Barbara Chafin explained that there was little comparison between their first small pastorate and the large one where they were when we had this conversation. And their first one was even different from many its size. "It was in a new area, with new people. There were few weddings and funerals. Families were young; children's departments flourished!" Most small churches are community centers; they house the neighborhood activities. If the Parent-Teacher's Organization wants to use the building, the pastor is the one who turns on the lights and locks up when the meeting is over.

Most ministers consider the rural and small town pastorates

stepping stones to the bigger churches and, of course, that *is* where you learn.

Actually, most churches are in the small bracket. Approximately three-fourths of our churches have 300 members or less. Your husband may pastor two part-time churches or work at some other job in addition to pastoring or leading the singing or directing the young people. A pastor who "has been there" says he feels that all seminary students should learn a trade or second profession so that they can be sure of supporting their families while they pursue their ministry career and work in these small churches.

But to think of your turn in small churches as temporary and *only* a stepping stone is to close the door on blessings. After all, striking a pose is not the same as conducting a policy. It is in these settings that you may be called on to do everything from preparing the food for the church supper to delivering a death message. One wife who has a reputation for being a fantastic cook gives credit to the ladies in small pastorates with whom she toiled to prepare food for suppers, dinners, banquets, picnics and teas. Another wife, who would have sworn she had no artistic ability, is great at making posters and illustrations because she *had* to make them in small churches where no one else could or would take on such assignments. Best of all, though—and many told me this—are those situations in which wives learned to talk with suffering people when no one else was there to do it, to visit in hospital rooms, to share scriptures.

Denise Fry said she took the advice of her pastor's wife, and when she and Matt got their first church, one with 216 members, she asked questions about people rather than about procedures or traditions. She worked in the children's area, so she would say to a lady of the church, "Tell me about Billy Smith." In the process, she would learn about Billy's family and all the people who touched his life. The ladies recognized her motivation and left her free to design and carry out her own children's program. Another young wife couldn't play the piano well but in her one-pianist church she became the number one substitute. Before they left that church, she had practiced hymns and children's songs so much during the week that her efforts were quite passable when she arrived at the next church.

Your tools may not be the greatest, but you'll learn to be innovative and conservative. I can understand being without proper tools. Recently I gathered up all my writing materials, filled the trunk of the car and came here to my hideaway to write. With everything spread on the table, I saw that I had left my dictionary and thesaurus at home! I can't spell the words on a grocery list without a dictionary, and my thesaurus is even more essential. So that was a week of rare mental exercise. You may be surprised at what genius you uncover when you are required to innovate.

"Of course, it's hard to hide in a small church," said Janet. "Everybody, but everybody, knows right where you are every minute. The way it is now—and we're in a medium-sized church—there are a few people who won't miss me even on Sunday nights."

So there's more pressure on you in small churches, but this pressure is the forerunner of motivation which prompts the action that develops the talent, so don't be too critical of pressure!

Opportunities to do your own thing or someone else's thing are better in larger churches. Your thing may be nothing more than that of a voting-but-non-participating member, or it may be leading the choir, the missionary society or an adult Bible class. Hopefully, you'll consolidate and relegate and leave some jobs for someone else.

Family therapist Ellen Jones says, "If wives have preconceived ideas about what they will and will not do, they limit what God can do through and for them." Or, as the adage goes, "The plans are man's; the odds are God's."

Though she never knew it, Eva Mae, one of my childhood friends, had great influence on my life. She had the best penmanship of anyone in school. How I envied her! Looking at my scribble at the end of fourth grade, I decided that I *would* learn to write like

Eva Mae; I would spend all summer at it. And I did. With her page in my autograph book as a pattern, I wrote day and night. I used all available Big Chief tablets from my brothers, then started in on magazines and newspapers, the back of Harry's Monopoly box, my dad's business receipts. If anyone put down a piece of paper, he or she could be sure of finding it covered with "Yvonne Cates"es. But by the time school started, one would have been hard put to tell my handwriting from Eva Mae's!

Starting where you are, build. You too may have to spend all summer on your enterprise. Or all winter. I wish for you an Eva Mae who sets high standards and who is available for advice and encouragement.

Janie's father was a preacher, so her mother had all the battle scars and the wisdom her role brings. Sharing this role with her mother has been and continues to be of inestimable benefit to Janie. Denise said, "I'm not sure I would have made it if it hadn't been for my pastor's wife whom I keep mentioning. She not only gave me a short course in what she called Pastor-ized-Wives-and-the-Milk-of-Human-Kindness, but she inspired me when I felt completely un-inspirable."

It takes more than book learning to know how to best contribute to your church. Early in her career, Ruth Porter's seminary degree worked more to her disadvantage than to her advantage. Or so she thought at the time. People would say to her, "Well, that's easy for you. You went to the seminary, you know all about that." Or, "I can't take that assignment, not with Ruth sitting there watching me." This situation was mentioned several times on our questionnaires. One wife, who described the same problem, proceeded to answer the next question, "What do you like best about being a pastor's wife?," by saying, "What I like best is learning to relate to members and seeing them relate to me, especially when they forget that I went to the seminary or that I'm the pastor's wife."

Ruth realizes now that her education was a good investment, that it helps her in ways she recognizes daily (and probably in ways she doesn't recognize) and stands her in good stead for professional employment down the line if she wants it.

When I asked wives which courses they wish they had had in school, a leading answer was *typing*. My sister-in-law Virginia has been married to her preacher-teacher husband for forty years, and it seems to us that every time we've had a letter or phone call from her, she has been typing a paper for Alan. Obviously, he is glad she learned to type. No doubt Virginia would be in great demand at the seminary where Alan teaches if she were to hang out her typing shingle. Cathy's voice lessons have enriched David's pastorates as she has sung solos and led in the music programs. Paula Grisham learned sign language as a part of her degree in Speech Therapy and is using it now to minister to a growing group of hearing-impaired people in their current pastorate.

And just as you help your husband, he will help you to learn the art of shepherding: making house calls and hospital calls, meeting new people, learning to listen and to respond.

During the last minutes before Cathy's father went into the operating room to have heart surgery, the family gathered around his bed and David led them in prayer. Later, Cathy said that one of the neat things about being a minister or a minister's wife is that "at times like that, it's instinctive to pray, and it's expected of you and, after all, someone needs to pray."

My church has a program on Tuesday mornings that teaches conversational English and creative classes to 200 international women. Another of our church programs ministers to out-of-town cancer patients at the medical center, providing housing, transportation, companionship and emotional support to hundreds of families each year. Both of these projects were begun because of the concern and ingenuity of a few women. These ladies are not ministers' wives and yet they are no different. Your church needs your creativity and initiative and you may need to get out of your sanctified rut.

My friend Shirley, who was four feet, ten and a half inches tall, said that when you are short, you have to accept the fact that your nose will always rest on hymnals when you sing in church, that taller people aren't about to hold a song book low enough for your eyes. Sometimes we have to live with frustration or hold our own song books. Having concepts and talents that you're unable to use is as disconcerting as being overwhelmed with responsibilities.

"I have sat in meetings," said Janet, "in which the process and content were restrained because of my presence, my being the pastor's wife and all. And yet I had said so much at that point that I felt I could not say more." So Janet declines to be on church committees; she feels the members need the "freedom of my absence."

A group was discussing the awkwardness of handling church business with the pastor's wife present. First, they felt somewhat disloyal if they disapproved her presentations because, all said and done, she is the pastor's wife. Then there were times when they would like to be able to explain to her that maybe she didn't understand exactly, that her vantage point is different, because she is a staff member really instead of a lay member. And finally there is always the fear that she will go home and report the proceedings to her husband.

Regardless of the lack of justification for such feelings, you need to be aware of these attitudes. You need also to put yourself in the place of these women and see if you too wouldn't have the same apprehensions. There is work enough to be done in churches without having to put yourself in a competitive situation with members. Denise is in charge of arranging or arranging-for flowers in the sanctuary for Sundays. "That's a fairly safe job. Most people won't complain about God's beautiful creations even if they are lopsided and somber. And if someone comes up and wants to take over my job, I'll miss it, but I won't go into mourning about it." Ruth teaches a class of young wives, most of whom are having babies, so she has no time to even think about another job in the church. Almost every week there's a hospital visit to make, a baby to enroll, meals for new parents to be coordinated (members do most of the cooking and delivering of food to homes), not to mention a lesson to prepare for Sunday morning.

It doesn't take much rebuffing to prompt some wives to cut themselves off completely from church responsibilities. But be assured that this not only is less than your reasonable service, but it is an impediment to the work of the church, your husband's prosperity and your emotional well-being.

Ruth Truman writes in her book that you're not just a minister's wife; "instead you are Mary Smith, Christian person. If it helps, introduce yourself as Mary Smith, period. Feel insecure? Good! Now you have to perform; you have to emerge."[1]

A missionary wife whom I met at a retreat said that when she and her husband were on furlough from the mission field, she enjoyed sitting in a Sunday School class so much that she could see how it could be a real temptation to do nothing *but* that in an urban church situation. And Ruth, with her class of young marrieds, believes teachers—"pastors wives included"—should have sabbaticals. However, Ruth would do something else during that time, like work in the library or visit for the Cradle Roll Department. She says she is skeptical of wives who flaunt their "freedom to do nothing." She has known ministers' wives who have gone to work solely to avoid daytime church activities, and most of them have no qualms about telling you so. Janie says that the minister's wife, even if she has an outside job, "needs to be active in her church just as any other professional is active. No more, no less." Of course, mothers with small children have to determine priorities, and those with dependent parents or invalid family members have special complications.

Then you've probably heard the story of the wife who liked to work in her yard—every day. She told herself and everyone else that it was therapy: it was her way of communing with God, being with His creations. But she added that people made her feel guilty; they would see her in her garden and wonder why she, the pastor's wife, was not at the meeting at the church and how she managed to have so much time to tend her flowers. She was tempted just to stay inside the house and never go out where they could see her—that would show them!

Cynics have never built cathedrals, they say—flower gardens maybe and clean homes, but not churches.

When Sarah and her husband left a loving and beloved congregation to accept a new position, she wrote a letter to the church. which was published in their weekly bulletin. In it she said, "Thank you for the privilege of teaching the Bible. Thank you for opportunity of service through the mission organizations. Thank you for being able to praise God in song, for the honor of working with college students. Thank you for caring for our grandson in the nursery, for the flowers in the sanctuary, for kind words, for loving us." Another wife expressed her gratitude for having learned how to stand on her feet, speak "in public" and even say grace out loud!

Results of a study by a group of ministers' wives list eight future challenges for our churches:

1. Dealing with negatives.
2. Traffic problems.
3. The computer age.
4. Influx of foreign cultures.
5. Apathy toward immorality.
6. Broken families.
7. Possible decreases in church growth.
8. Lack of available pastors.

These *are* challenges, and they are out there for your accepting.

When I was in college, I was intrigued with my French teacher's obsession of wanting to wake up in Paris thinking in French. She had traveled to France several times, but confessed to us that she always woke up thinking in English. Recently, after thirty years, I saw her again. I asked her if she had accomplished her dream. "Oh, yes," she said, "long ago. But it required many trips and many wakings-up."

Mrs. Westmoreland said it another way, remember? "Overcoming problems makes you stronger."

Time is a great teacher. With many wakings-up, you will soon find yourself busy and confident and strong-in-the-Lord.

NOTES

1. Ruth Truman, *Underground Manual for Ministers' Wives* (Nashville: Abingdon, 1974), p. 144.

Working with the People

Beside a road that our family travels often is a dilapidated building which we assume was once a sandwich shop or a barbecue stand. Looming high above it, still sturdy and intact, is its sign: "Sarge's Place." And every time I pass by what used to be Sarge's, I wonder why his business was less enduring than his sign, why such a strong announcement for something so temporary.

If we aren't careful, this could be a description of our work with people in the church; we need to watch that our sign doesn't outlast our project, that we are not remembered only for weak strategy and strong attack.

First of all, it is true that people—and you are no exception—need people. As a rule, I react most negatively to telephone sales pitches, but recently when I spent several days alone writing, I welcomed the voice of a saleswoman who wanted to re-roof my house. I'm sure it was the friendliest non-sale response she had ever had. You need the people of your church; they need you. It be-hooves you to learn to work together in love.

Janet remembers once, when she was very young, having said to her not-yet-a-pastor husband, "But, Tom, you make church work sound like dealing with just *people*, not God." He laughed and said, "Well, you certainly have to deal with people, all right. And any other work we could go into would mean getting involved with people. If I were a doctor or a lawyer, a businessman, teacher, anything. Church isn't just God." He mentioned something to the effect that she would learn in time that most problems are people-problems, in and out of the church.

David and Vera Mace, after their study of clergy marriages, reported: "Our investigations have consistently given us the im-pression that lay members of congregations are generally charitable and well disposed toward the minister and his family. In many churches, however, there exist certain members who, by their fault-finding and belligerence, communicate to the pastor, and particularly to his wife, an impression about the views and attitudes of the congregation that is largely or entirely inaccurate."[1]

I suggest that you place your major emphasis on the first sentence of that statement and keep in mind, from the second part, the words "certain members" and "largely or entirely inaccurate."

During my adult life, I have had six different pastors and I do not recall ever having heard anyone make a disparaging statement about any of my pastors' wives. I recounted this remarkable obser-vation to several people in an effort to convince myself that I had not been living with my head in the sand, being as how I read so much and hear so much about wives being maligned by their parishioners. My husband said he thought it was just that my particular friends have never gossiped about the pastor's wife. My sister-in-law said it probably was that people who might want to make negative remarks to me knew how I'd respond, that she knows it does happen because she sees little groups in her church who are "out to get the pastor's wife." A friend who was once a pastor's wife in a very small church said their members weren't even secretive about it; they criticized her to her face.

I remember the first time I realized that people talked about me, really put their thoughts about me into words. It wasn't because I'd heard gossip or anything like that; it was just one of those momentous thoughts. Ministers' wives live with this knowledge. They're told at the seminary it's going to happen, their husbands tell them to pay no attention to it, and their mothers tell them to consider the source. Still, as the Maces say, most church members are charitable and well disposed toward you.

Probably the minister's wife is no more victimized than is the president of the missionary society or the soprano in the choir or the pastor's secretary. Or, for that matter, the doctor's wife, the superintendent's wife or the officer's wife. As Kahlil Gibran said, to be enthroned is to be enslaved.

Even so, you still may have to learn how to handle gossip. One clever wife would respond to verbal pettiness with, "Well, we'll just have to refer that to the proper committee." Then one day she heard that the scuttlebutt around the church was that there was no need to tell anything to the preacher's wife, since "she'll just refer it to a committee!"

There will be times when you'd like to tell them good things about your husband or your children or even yourself, but you don't, for fear of being accused of bragging, then hearing the garbled message repeated to you.

Obviously, carrying tales is child's play: like the game of Gossip, it grows and takes on a new twist. As the proverb goes, "Whatsoever you know nothing of, thereof say nothing." Even listening puts you in a compromising position. Mrs. Westmoreland said she always prayed hard to forget things, things best not remembered.

How much you should know about the members of your church continues to be a matter of debate. How much information the pastor should take home to his family is another question. Often your husband will not confide in you because he knows such news will color the opinion of someone with whom you need to have good rapport. Denise had a close friend, a young woman with whom she worked on Sunday mornings. It was not until Denise and her husband moved from that city that she learned (from her husband) that this friend had been responsible for much of the recrimination that influenced them to look for new employment.

When he was in high school, one of our sons said you could always tell who the "brains" were at school because they'd go around with calculators in their belt loops. It's too bad we don't have such identification clues for the people of the church, a way to know where you stand with everyone, who the gossips are, the underminers, the malcontents. Yet if you could recognize your adversaries, you might be inclined to avoid them when actually they are the ones who need your friendship.

A Methodist pastor tells of a woman in his church who was a real nuisance to the entire congregation. One day a disgruntled member said to the pastor, "I wish that woman were a Baptist!" And the pastor said, "Oh, no, don't wish that. She is one of the most important people in this church. You see, if you can learn to love her, you can love everyone else."

Eugenia Price writes about the same theory. In one of her early books she recalls the time she prayed for patience, that her project for the month was to learn to be long-suffering and understanding. When she came home from school the next day, her mother told her that her aunt, the unbearable, talkative, bossy one, was coming for a visit. Genie's first impulse was to groan. Then she realized that here was her perfect arena for learning patience!

I asked Janie what she considered the biggest problem she had worked through, as a minister's wife. As usual, her answer came quickly: "Learning to work with people even though I'm angry at them. You have to learn not to get up and leave every time there's a problem. Growing means hurting sometimes; it means you *win* battles and you *lose* battles—there's no way *you* can be right every time, so why should you expect it of others?"

Many ministers' wives, strange as it may seem, have trouble learning to give and receive with grace, and seem especially to have trouble with the receiving. It seems to me that every minister's wife should have a large food freezer to take care of the cakes, pies, cookies and casseroles that are brought by her house or handed to her and her husband at church. One Sunday morning, several weeks after Christmas, our pastor thanked me for the pie he and the family had enjoyed that week. I walked away thinking he had confused my gift with someone else's; then I realized that his well-organized wife had simply parceled out the holiday goodies, which she had stored in her freezer to make them last longer—and the pie I had taken by at Christmas was eaten in February.

Even though you may have more Chicken Cacciatore than you can say grace over and the baskets of fresh fruit spoil before they can be eaten, it is important that your members feel free to give you gifts. They need tangible ways to show their love. And they bask in the knowledge of having pleased you; they feel gratified on hearing or reading your thank-yous.

In a dinner conversation one evening, the friends with whom we were dining told us with exuberance about the most unusual gift ever given to them. Early in December, a couple in their church had invited them for dinner on the evening of December 18th. It was a busy month, but they had managed to keep the evening free. During the afternoon of December 18th, the hostess called to say, "Don't dress up. Build a fire in your fireplace and turn down the lights —*we* are coming to *your* place." At 6:00 o'clock in walked the husband and wife with a gourmet meal for two which they set on a table (linen cloth, candles, the whole bit) before the fireplace, then left with the admonition "When you finish, don't worry about the dishes. We'll come back in the morning and get them." It was unexpected bliss to have an evening at home during the rush of the holidays.

Prayer is a very special gift between the pastor's family and the congregation, and you will grow in prayer. One wife said it was much easier for her to pray for others than to let them pray for her.

"Their prayers always came through to me sounding like I was a burden, though that was not at all the way they were intended."

Janie said the people of the church should see in the minister's wife a model of prayer life.

"How," I asked, "do they *see* such a pattern?"

"They see it because she says 'I'll pray for you' and because she says 'thank you for praying for me' and because she really does pray and they know she does."

The minister and his wife do not always learn in the seminary how to cope with difficult relationships in the church. All churches are different and all people are different. By the same token, they do not always learn how to deal with their own emotions: anger, impatience, disappointment, retaliation, greed. It would be a magical seminary course that would teach you how to hold your tongue or how to avoid being jealous of those you consider more charming and talented than you. Alice Taylor says that what she often sees is the minister's wife who, "little by little, forms a hard shell around herself, like the turtle, where she may hide until the storm is over." She says she has found that the best way to deal with "cantankerous souls" is to heed the advice of Luke to love your enemies, do good to them and pray for them. "It works." she says. "We know it does, because we have tried it."[2]

Whenever the subject of gentleness versus force comes up in our family, someone always recalls the time Cousin Bobby slapped at the mosquito inside his car and wrecked the whole windshield in the process. Church alliances are more valuable than windshields, and the same principle applies.

Besides being gentle, you learn to smile, then graduate to laughter. "You don't just cry about and with people," said Janet; "there's a time to laugh too. It's Biblical and it's necessary. People need to see you laugh, to know that you aren't one of those pious-and-perturbed preacher's wives."

A church member was late to a bridal shower and the only chair left was next to her pastor's wife. "I really didn't want to sit there because I was afraid I would say all the wrong things. I didn't know how to be with a minister's wife except at church. But she was so funny and so much like everyone else that I forgot she was someone special."

All of us have been brought up with the counsel that, as Christians, we should be available to those among us in need. Ministers' wives especially feel this tug, and yet your sphere of involvement is not unlike that of any other member.

One wife opened an antique shop not only because she liked antiques but also because she wanted "a different look at life, to meet those on the outside and, for lack of a better word, *witness* to them." A family therapist, working with her husband in a pioneer church area of the Northeast, is using her degree in her own counseling center. From the major elements of emotional fitness to everyday management "such as entertaining, budgeting and grooming," she communicates guidelines to fledgling minister's wives. Lois Nabors has been a fifth-grade teacher "forever." She teaches scriptures through mathematical equations and Christian principles "all day long."

Yet working away from home not only limits some areas of availability but has drawbacks which I would not have detected. "You have to realize," said Janet, "that even though some of us choose to have outside jobs, we give up a lot. Our friends don't call us as much because they're afraid of encroaching on our time. Those who don't work grow away from us because they do things in the daytime that don't include us. And things like, well, you see that the flower bed needs working or you'd like to bake a cake, but there just isn't time."

Carol Wilson says it hits her when she's driving to work and she sees housewives walking the dogs, pushing baby carriages and going to the grocery store at 8:30 in the morning.

("But people who work miss some grungy things too," said Janet. "They avoid annoying phone calls and soap operas and wasted days.")

Still, most of the "blessings" recounted to me, it seems, had to do with filling in and helping out at unexpected times in unexpected places. One wife stayed up all night long with a teen-age girl who had been raped. "She went home calm and ready to sleep." Another wife received a letter from a high school girl "thanking me for sharing my husband" the night before when the girl was involved in a near-assault. A frightened and cold out-of-state young man stopped at the Carl Nelson home one rainy November afternoon. They found dry clothes for him while Martha Nelson put his things in the dryer. Then, over hot chocolate and crackers, "we talked about religion and life," put him up for the night and sent him on his way the next morning, nourished and revived. Alice Taylor tells about the time she handled an emergency when her husband couldn't be located, with the realization later that "the Lord had placed me in this situation at the correct moment." Not only did she take care of a grieving man whose wife had just died, but she spent three hours on the phone delivering the death message to relatives and friends.

"Sometimes I get angry at the church," said Denise, "but how do you *fight* the church?"

How do you? How do you get back at people for keeping your husband from you, for invading your privacy, for ignoring you and criticizing you?

First of all, you remind yourself that it goes with the territory, that it comes from being a wife, a church member, an intelligent, observant person—a human being, if you please, with feelings and emotions. As the song goes, "Feeling sad, feeling low, but, thank God, I'm feeling."

Then, as they say in the business world, "when all else fails, read your memo." You'll find more dealing-with-the-church messages in the New Testament than you'll be able to read during any one irate spell. Prayer will take the edge off your fire; Christian fellowship will revamp your attitude.

Keep in mind that even though there probably is a disconcerting power structure in your church and little bands of grumblers, you are not the only one to have to deal with them. While you are home letting off steam, you are joined by deacons, Sunday School teachers, staff members and secretaries sitting in other houses licking wounds.

So, with your whole armor, go forth. A California minister's wife said that when she moved from the East Coast to the West Coast, a new world was opened to her—or not opened, actually. "In Bible-belt areas, you're just supposed to walk around town and be a blessing to everybody, but out here they don't know you from Adam, and even if you tell them you're a minister or a minister's wife, well, so what?"

One pastor has a "Formula for Getting Along With People" that he passes on to his congregation:

1. Love magnifies the person.
2. Love volunteers itself.
3. Love makes commitments.
4. Love creates a context for moral and ethical seriousness.
5. Love makes demands.
6. Love is realistic.
7. Love creates a basis for starting over.

My sister-in-law Marguerite used her own brand of ingenuity in getting along with people, particularly children. At my house one day, she observed me cutting the brown spots from bananas. She said, "Oh, don't let Bobby see you do that; he thinks the brown spots are what make them good." Bobby also thought warm Cokes were better than cold ones and he thought knots in shoestrings were neat.

So use your ingenuity to advantage and keep your boot straps in order, knots and all, and even though your landing may not be a smooth one, rejoice if it's at least controlled. Working with people in the church really can be a blessing—for you and for them.

Those who shared their ups and downs with me say it really is worth the effort.

NOTES

1. David and Vera Mace, *What's Happening to Clergy Marriages?* (Nashville: Abingdon, 1980), pp. 53, 54.
2. Alice Taylor, *How to Be a Minister's Wife and Love It* (Grand Rapids, MI: Zondervan, 1968), p. 116.

Standing by Your Man

Anne Morrow Lindbergh wrote to a friend, "Apparently I am going to marry Charles Lindbergh. Don't wish me happiness—wish me courage and strength and a sense of humor. I will need them all."[1]

And you will need them all, married to your man. You will need courage just to get up some mornings, strength for the day and a sense of humor when your feet are tired and your head is throbbing.

The first step is always acceptance. Hopefully, this procedure took place before you married, as much as was possible. You accepted the fact that he is or was to be a minister and that, married to him, you'd be a minister's wife. Very simple. But seminary isn't "the calling" and certainly isn't the same as being on the field. During student days you had friends around the corner in your apartment unit and, when you walked on campus, you were surrounded by peers engaged in like pursuits. Now you live in a world where people come in all ages, sizes and persuasions.

No doubt, you have noticed that your husband is in a precarious profession, that sometimes the center just doesn't hold. And there are those who say it's hardest on the wife. But in this chapter we're looking at the husband and dealing with ways to loosen the clerical collar and comfort him both in and out of the church.

Most of the criticism from church members will not reach your ears. Or his. It's a bit difficult to deal with something you don't hear.

"Most of what we've experienced," said Ruth, "is more rejection than blatant disapproval. Like not including us at some gathering or replacing Steve's suggestion with one from someone else. For example, there was the time Steve worked so hard planning a men's retreat at the encampment grounds. He and I both spent hours on it and Steve felt so good about everything. Then, the week before, the church board decided to have the whole thing at the church hall because some of the men didn't want to drive thirty miles and they thought they'd have a better attendance by staying in town!"

"How did it work out?"

"Oh, you know Steve. He went on as if nothing had happened and said I should do likewise. They probably did have more people there. Steve says they'll plan the next one at a better time of the year and get the publicity started sooner. It didn't bother Steve as much as it did me."

Most husbands manage the day-to-day pros and cons of church life better than their wives do. The problem lies in standing back and watching someone you love being mistreated. If you were in the middle of the fray, it would be easier. If Ruth had been with the men when they discussed the changes, and then later, with them at the meeting, she could have treated the situation with the same aplomb that Steve used and not be going around, even now, blaming the church elders.

So take a clue from your husband. If he can pass it off, you can pass it off—and, like Steve, go on to the next thing.

There was a time in Ruth's life—long before the men's retreat incident—when she would go to bed at night asking herself "where is he?" and wake up in the morning asking "where was he?" "Looking back, I realize those days didn't last long really, but, at the time, it seemed forever. I see younger wives going through that now, their first pastorates and all, and I wish I could relieve them of some of their anxiety."

"What would you tell them?"

"Oh, I'd get pretty preachy, I'm afraid. Like, don't grumble to your husband; he's doing his best. And stay busy with your thing. Make some friends, laugh a lot. That's the way you can help him the most."

A business associate of my husband told of visiting one of his young employees in the hospital where he had been taken with a very serious illness. As the friend stood in the corridor with the young wife, her assessment of her circumstances was, "I may be a widow at twenty-eight!" Our friend observed that her concern was turned inward.

Be sure your thoughts are not just for yourself. As best you can, walk in your husband's shoes. Your defense of him should be at home, not at the church; he can handle his own defense—and he doesn't need to have to answer for you too. William Hulme writes that ministers are often partisan when it comes to their wives and this can compound their problems. "If she is unhappy because she is lonely, her husband feels somewhat responsible....The minister may find it hard not to resent the congregation and the community that leaves his wife feeling left out."[2]

He is likely to react this way to any wife-type problem: a slight that you report to him, crying in your coffee cup about the fears of the day, bounding home in anger from a stormy women's meeting. If he ignores or belittles your complaints, he has problems at home; if he retaliates, he has problems at the church.

If the first step in helpmeethood is acceptance, the second one has to be commitment—the determination to make it! After all, tolerance and coping are not the same.

Many recent reports have come out on dual-career marriages and the need for an effective support system. One study claimed that marriage partners "may want to be supportive, but they just may not be available when the other needs recreation, relaxation or just a friendly ear."[3]

A doctor was explaining his discouragement in dealing with uncooperative patients. "Often I come home at night," he said, "too exhausted to talk to my wife and children. I've expended all my energy in talking to those patients who return as fat as ever, who keep on smoking, drinking and never taking one bit of advice. Sometimes I wish I were just a surgeon."[4]

If it's true of the doctor, it's true of the minister.

Your husband's need right now may be to have you more available.

Since we perceive that it is not good for man—or woman—to be alone and since we know the mutual build-up is needed, how is it that we so often stage our holy wars and make separate retreats? Or retreat without even so much as a council?

Often this pattern of confrontation, or no confrontation, becomes routine while fellow-husband is in school and has made some spur-of-the-moment promise about "when I graduate and go to work, we'll have more time," and you're sitting there now wondering what happened to those after-graduation prophecies. There's one thing about being married to an accountant; there were never any predictions about next year's being easier. And if your husband expected shorter working hours as a pastor, someone has been feeding him propaganda. My husband's birthday, coming in the middle of the public accounting busy season, seldom got observed during the first ten years of our marriage. I can still see me sitting in the dining room befriending a tiny birthday cake at 2:00 in the morning and hearing the annual response from my haggard husband when he walked in, "Why don't we save it till another time?"

Any workman worthy of his hire will at least begin his career putting in long hours. At that point, the much-used and over-used "quality time" exhortation is in order. One of those nights when you're propping your eyes open waiting for the turn of his key in the lock, read about some successful men and women who once were where you are now. Then spend what daytime hours you find unscheduled to brush up on information that makes you an authority of sorts on at least one subject that you can impart to him when your reunion does take place. One wife said she came well trained as a minister's wife because she grew up in a politician's home and "when your dad is constantly running for office, you don't dare lag behind on *any*thing."

Janie says it helps to remember "who your husband is," that he really is a man called apart. A study on new pastorates reveals what wives already suspected, that the job "creates a critically important teachable moment—both by him and the church. It is a time of high energy and motivation, a time of excitement and fright."[5]

A husband who comes home high on this motivation and excitement to clash with an unmotivated, unexcited wife is in for an emotional letdown, to say the least. One minister who experienced the highs of clergy life and the lows of married life said, "She just never gets excited enough. I could walk in and tell her we're taking a trip to the Riviera and she'd say, 'That's nice.'" I see ministers' wives weekly who appear to find great pleasure in their roles; I can't imagine that they don't "get excited enough."

The daughter of a prominent Tennessee pastor described her mother as the busiest worker-organizer-women's leader in the state until she married, then "she became a full-time preacher's wife, a role in which she was totally happy. Her only complaint came when my father went off to war (as a chaplain) at a time when her four children were very small. Besides, she didn't believe in war."

Many sons and daughters of ministers have told me, using almost identical words, "My father could never have been a pastor without my mother." It may be that there is no wife behind *every* successful minister, but the odds certainly seem to favor you. My husband and sons who sat glued to the TV during the World Series playoffs thought they saw and heard the whole thing, but they missed the crux of it—the explanation from Cecil Cooper on how he came to hit that winning run. "I looked out," he said, "and saw my wife's face and I said to myself, 'I've just gotta get one!'"

The ultimate in support and commitment comes from a statement attributed to the wife of Dr. W. R. White, former president of Baylor University and before that a pastor. She said, "Billy's praying and I'm packing." You too will know when to start packing and, like Mrs. White, be ready for the next adventure.

With acceptance and commitment behind you, you move on to the nitty-gritty of living under the same roof, when, of course, you're both under the same roof. A recommendation from a pastoral support group cited two critical needs for ministers: consistent encouragement and feedback-and-evaluation. You should encourage your husband to participate in such mutual support groups, but he needs a similar sounding board at home, a climate for both of you to talk out problems and ideas. For example, even though he will say that the consultations that go on behind his closed office door (including those with women) are private affairs, he would do well to heed two warnings from hundreds of ministers who learned through the grief process: (1) maybe the door shouldn't be closed in the first place, and (2) better to talk it over with your wife than to go down in defeat. One pastor said, "My office door is never closed unless I am in there alone. Opened doors deter hanky panky and keep the counseling just that—counseling." Most husbands who have become involved romantically with their female clients will tell you that if their wives had known about it, things would never have gone so far. Touché!

Ena Naunton has written about the domestic problems of clergymen and she harps on this shepherd-and-lost-lamb syndrome. She calls it a vocational hazard, but, more often than not, a self-imposed one. The hazard is "the woman in the congregation who sees the man in the pulpit as something more than her pastor. This can be either amusing or devastating for the pastor's wife." Ena tells about Roxy Dear, a pastor's wife and daughter of divorced parents, who had her formula for dealing with women she felt were "after him." She wouldn't really attack the woman, but she would be especially supportive of her husband and make him—and the "other woman"—aware that she, the wife, was number one. Elaine Schofield can understand how women succumb to the charms of her husband, "but I'm the one who's got him and I plan to keep him."[6]

It's a constant barrage of women: secretaries, staff members and wives, troubled mothers of teen-agers, elderly members bent on mothering him, choir members, enamored college students. Only by locking him up all week and putting him behind glass at 11:00 on Sunday morning can you keep him unscathed. So the solution *has* to lie in the trappings of home.

Home should be a place where secrets can die their natural deaths. If he confides in you, it means you're the stopgap; if he wanted it announced, he'd use the church bulletin. My introduction into the coterie of accountants'-wives-and-how-they-grow was punctuated by a parable from the wife of the partner-in-charge of my husband's accounting firm, who explained that her husband told her nothing about the goings-on at the office and, in answer to all her inquiries, would say, "Doris, what you don't know you can't tell." Needless to say, there was very little I knew, therefore very little to tell. It's easier that way, but it limits our involvement and the opportunities to be supportive. Maybe also it's different with a church vocation; clients' names—meaning church members—are not private and interactions are not kept under lock and key. One thing is for sure, your husband *will* have a sounding board, or he will go one of two directions: he'll hit the ceiling or the floor. It would be good if you could step in here and be more to him than just another pretty face.

Psychiatrist Louis McBurney has studied the phenomenon of the *lack* of anger in the parsonage. This may not relate to you at all, this absence of anger, but it's worth some space here for those souls who avoid conflict at all costs, who do not express even righteous indignation. According to the McBurney report, the reason anger is so "assiduously"—that's his word, not mine—avoided is because, in the first place, we have not been taught how to express it; it frightens us and leaves us feeling sinful. Then "anger induces deep within our beings the primitive impulse to react aggressively…fear of losing control demands the lid be screwed on tightly and never lifted off."[7]

Dr. McBurney cautions that the walls built between people by unexpressed anger are far more destructive than is direct confrontation. Anger should not be stockpiled but should be worked out-and-through by means of healthy interchange.

Certainly it shouldn't be stockpiled until Sunday morning, when you both go to church mad. Which is the first of a list of handling anger guidelines I've collected from experienced ministers' wives. The remainder of the list follows:

2. Speak up; don't make him have to "read" you.
3. Don't nag; come out with it, once and for all.
4. If you're mad at God instead of at your husband, tell him so—both Hims.
5. Never, never argue in public. That means church too.
6. Don't criticize his accomplishments—or lack of accomplishments.
7. Remember that sometimes you may be the scapegoat—but you don't want him to lash out at the church members, do you?
8. Be sure the climate is good for *him* to blow *his* top—you shouldn't have all the fun.
9. Don't throw things. Especially if you live in a parsonage.
10. Always bring arguments to conclusion—not just on Saturday nights, but Tuesday nights and Thursday noons and all week. Never leave an argument dangling or festering.

A husband's physical needs are more easily distinguished than his other needs. If he, like Potiphar, "concerns himself with nothing but the food he eats," then you know to heat up the meat loaf. But when he sits in the Lazy Boy with that faraway ogle in his eye, you may be hard put to decipher the message. You may think he's dreaming of you and the new silk sheets when what he's actually thinking about is the prayer breakfast for Friday morning. And as sure as you think you have him all sized up as having some deep-seated emotional psychosis, you find out he's worried about the bank account. All of which is to say that men are extremely hard to figure out on certain days. But you, the prudent-wife-from-the-Lord must try, you really must try. Start with his obvious needs: Mondays off, a check-up at the doctor's office, time with his friends, vacation, a trip home, help with Sunday's sermon, a diet, a shoulder to lean on. Then go from there.

Take the Mondays-off idea, which really isn't a bad one at all. Monday is a logical day for the minister to relax, unwinding from the busy Sabbath before rewinding for the week ahead. But Monday is also the day when most people are refreshed from their weekend and are in gear for the work week. So they start in on Monday morning contacting the pastor with questions and suggestions from Sunday and with plans for the week. If Monday is not his choice day, help him find another one—and use your devices to get him to putter in the yard or go fishing or whatever takes his mind off his saint-watching for the day. Janet said that when the church "gave" Tom a day off—"he would never have lifted a finger to get it"—and insisted that he use it, she drove him out of town for the first two Thursdays "to help get him started on the habit." If it's true for the banker or the lawyer, it's true for the minister: "The schedule is made for the man and not the man for the schedule."

Many ministers are sadly lacking in close friendships. One deacon said, "What I wish most for my pastor is that he had one close, really close, best friend." Fortunately, strides are being made in developing support groups for clergymen, fellow pastors of various denominations who get together to brainstorm and compare notes and laugh and cry with each other. This is often easier and wiser than singling out men from your own church for companionship. I have found a common, therapeutic and happy situation developing in ministers' families, particularly in the cities. Little dinner groups of pastors and wives are appearing all over town and bringing a much-needed social outlet for church professionals.

Terry Hekker deals with meeting husbands' needs in her book *Ever Since Adam and Eve*. She says we could use a consumer's guide for the care and feeding of husbands, that there are things the experts don't tell you, like "You don't prove you love your wife by bringing home posies but by taking out the garbage; and you don't prove you love a man by going to bed with him but by getting up with him."[8]

When David and Vera Mace did their survey of ministers and wives, they found that one out of every five couples admitted needing help in the area of sex. Two out of three checked as a need "time alone together." Many couples find help in these two facets of their lives by attending marriage enrichment retreats or by getting away on frequent mini-vacations. One pastor said his marriage has improved in recent years "because we have observed good marriages in our church and have seen weak ones crumble."

Your man is different from all the others and you probably know him as well as or better than he knows himself. If he's a perfectionist or a workaholic, you probably are learning to live with that. We are told that the perfectionist tends to run himself down in an unconscious hope of getting others to build him up. The workaholic is not long swayed by any slowdowns brought to bear on his life, yet he is low on self-esteem most of the time.

You've noticed, haven't you, that the people in your church worship your husband more than they do God sometimes and speak to you of their pastor's many virtues? So here you are living alone with this angelic creature who appears to you to be quite normal, except for the days when he falls short of that, and you try to look at him through the eyes of his adoring sisters-in-Christ and wish somehow they could see him now. You must resist the urge to tell them he picks his teeth at meals and screams—honestly and truly, he does—at his children. You serve no good purpose in saying to them, "Oh, he's not all you've made him out to be."

The wife of one gregarious husband has to remind him often, when they go as guests to a party or a dinner, "Remember, you're not in charge tonight." Gina says that when her husband is out of *his* element, like at a social gathering, he clams up like you wouldn't believe. "You'd never recognize him as that poised pulpiteer of Sunday mornings."

Times away together—even if he clams up or takes charge—are vital to your marriage and your health. It may take real wizardry to fit togetherness into your schedule, especially togetherness alone. One young wife says that since she works Monday through Friday and her husband, the pastor of a small rural church, works on Sundays—and studies and visits on Saturdays—they take frequent one- and two-day vacations during the week. Before they found a workable plan, she was frustrated because of her husband's busyness on Saturdays and their lack of time for relaxing. It was difficult to even get his attention. She kept saying to herself, "He doesn't like me on Saturdays."

Which is a switch; most wives feel unliked on Sundays and it seems to be common practice for husbands and wives to avoid being at the same places at the same times on Sundays for fear of stepping on each others' toes, so to speak.

"I'm really the neglected wife until church is over on Sunday nights," said Denise. "Afternoon is nap time; then it's back to the church for the evening activities. When we get home on Sunday nights, we drop in our tracks. But we haven't upset each other during the day, and I guess that's worth something."

Sunday is absolutely not the day for criticizing sermons; most wives know that. (They must teach that warning in seminary.) Janie said Bob preached many sermons accompanied by dangling coins in his pockets. "He just couldn't remember to keep his hands out of his pockets—or to empty them beforehand." Emptying pockets is certainly a less complicated solution to faux-pas-in-the-pulpit than many wives have to deal with. "I am sure," said one minister, "that if my wife had chosen to critique my sermons on the way home from church every Sunday, our marriage would not have lasted all these years." Wives tell of wanting to slip under the pew as husbands stand in front of congregations and make grammatical errors, lose their places in their notes, fumble for scripture passages, mispronounce words—and yet these wives know they serve by having a relaxed countenance and a straight back.

The wife of a college-town pastor wrote notes to her husband listing errors he may have made in his sermon; these notes she left on his desk so he'd see them on Monday morning. By the time he got home on Monday nights, he had forgotten about the criticism, and yet his wife had been able to get her message across.

One young wife said, "I wish there were a way to offer constructive criticism while still accepting our husbands for the preachers they are, not expecting them to measure up to someone else's standards."

You may get the opportunity, if you choose to call it an opportunity, of stepping in your husband's shoes sometime. In *Papa's Wife*, Thyra Ferre Bjorn tells of the time her mother did just that, back in the days when women, like children, were seen and not heard or heard from. "It was the first time Papa had missed preaching his Sunday sermon in twelve years. The deacons were so impressed with Mama's rendition of Papa's sermon that they told Papa, 'The church is mighty lucky to have two preachers.'"[9] Donna Sinclair says that one of the unique things about a minister's wife is that often she *can* fill in for her husband; she couldn't do that if her husband were an engineer or a surgeon.

One of your husband's most difficult times will be when he must comfort his grieving people. When these days come, writes Martha Nelson, wives must remember that "it is impossible for the minister to continue to give strong support to families following crisis because scarcely has one crisis passed before another crops up. There is definitely a limit to the number of persons to whom one can minister in depth at any given time."[10] Ardelle Clemons says it is vital to remember that a pastor really does go through a grief situation with these people; he must and does share their sorrow.

So how does a wife help? Certainly not by ignoring the situation or begrudging the time he spends with the family that is grieving or by asking too many questions while he's trying to think through a funeral service.

I asked Carol Wilson, "What is the most difficult experience you have had as a minister's wife?"

"My most difficult experience," said Carol, "turned out to be my number one—well, who counts?—lesson-learner as a minister's wife. My uncle had died. This was a very special uncle, like a father to me, really. I was crushed and I knew my mother would be absolutely devastated. I needed Charles, and Mother needed Charles. But one of the leading members of our church had died just a few hours before we got the call about my uncle and, of course, Charles had to stay in town for that funeral, and I had to go alone to my uncle's funeral. I had every emotion you can imagine fighting inside me. I was worried about leaving the children, about consoling Mother, about not being with Charles back home. I was grieving for myself and my relatives. And I was angry at Charles, I guess, and at the circumstances that had both these deaths coming at the same time. I had a lot of time to think on the way there and back, and I learned a great deal in what was my first *close* touch with death. I learned that God really does give you strength and that I have resources I didn't know I had and that if anything ever happened to Charles, I could make it. All the courses in Death-and-Dying could never have taught me that!"

Brooks Faulkner writes that handling stress is what the ministry is all about, that "it's a demanding job that drives the minister again and again into the presence of Jesus. He alone can empower and equip us for the scores of tensions involved in doing his will and leading his church."[11]

So be assured that your husband has his source of strength and that what he needs most from you are your prayers and your empathy. Or, in the words of one wife, you have to grow up, painful though it may be, and share in some of his sorrows—not just his joys.

Learning to manage the times of sorrow flows over into other areas. It helps in facing unknowns, in making decisions, dealing with fears, handling disappointments, even being alone. "He needs to know," said Carol, "that if the job doesn't work out or if he makes a mess of the sermon, he doesn't have to worry about me too."

Vernon and I were having dinner with Doris and Jess Moody. It was the first time the two men had seen each other since they were roommates in college. After the exchange of amenities, Jess looked us over, then turned to Vernon and said, "One thing is for certain, friend; you and I both *over*-married." Hopefully, your husband also over-married and feels that you are his greatest earthly asset. You know in your heart of hearts that he needs all the help he can get. There are times when, as the words of the country-western song put it, all he "can count on are my fingers." Be sure he can count on you.

NOTES

1. Adela Rogers St. John, *Some Are Born Great* (New York: Signet Books, 1974), p. 271.
2. William E. Hulme, *Your Pastor's Problems* (Minneapolis: Augsburg, 1977), p. 111.
3. Meme Drumwright, "The Dual-Career Marriage," *Baylor Line*, June 1981, p. 24.

4. Dr. Peter Steincrohn, "Doctor Has Little Time For Unheeding Patient," *New Orleans Times-Picayune*, Oct. 1982.

5. *Commission on Ministry Report*, Baptist State Convention of North Carolina, Nov. 1981, p. 20.

6. Ena Naunton, "The Domestic Challenge of Clergy Life," *Houston Post*, Aug. 3, 1981, sec. B, p. 2.

7. Louis McBurney, *Every Pastor Needs a Pastor* (Waco, TX: Word Books, 1977), p. 103.

8. Terry Hekker, *Ever Since Adam and Eve* (New York: Wm. Morrow & Co., 1979), p. 120.

9. Thyra Ferre Bjorn, *Papa's Wife* (New York; Toronto: Rinehart & Co., 1955), p. 77.

10. Martha Nelson, *This Call We Share* (Nashville: Broadman, 1977), p. 78.

11. Brooks Faulkner, *Stress in the Life of the Minister* (Nashville: Convention Press, 1981), p. 140.

Your Own Four Walls

> Man was dreadfully wild. He didn't even begin to be tame till he met the Woman, and she told him that she did not like living in his wild ways. She picked out a nice dry cave, instead of a heap of wet leaves to lie in; and she lit a nice fire of wood at the back of the cave; and she hung a dried wild-horse skin across the opening of the cave, and she said, "Wipe your feet, dear, when you come in, and now we'll keep house."
>
> —Rudyard Kipling, "The Cat Who Walked by Himself"

Our evolution from the prehistoric cave wife is dramatic, to say the least, and yet our kinship to the Woman is not so far removed. Our urban version of the cave still finds us using our own devices to obtain comfort and cleanliness and privacy and domesticity.

Or, as Terry Hekker put it, ever since Adam and Eve, women have spent their lives caring for men, their dwellings and their children. "Only the tools have changed. The bunch of twigs which swept the cave gave way to the electric broom, but women were still wielding the handle. The animal roasting over an open fire gave way to the microwave oven, but women were still being blamed for burning the roast."[1]

"Once," said Janet, "I was going from dirty sink to unmade beds singing 'Take from our lives the strain and stress, and let our ordered lives confess the beauties of your peace' knowing full well that if the beauty of God's peace is dependent on my ordered life, God's world is in trouble."

Alyene Porter's mother came as near to leading an orderly life as any minister's wife I've read about or heard about. Alyene wrote that she cooked meals, made clothing for eight, directed church plays, taught mission study courses and "still, at any hour, she found the time and energy for feeding the hunger of a childish soul. Her voice with the low, sweet ring of a bell intoning words from the Bible, or from our favorite story books, created an aura of security which no force from an outer world could penetrate." This fantastic woman once told a neighbor, "I never feel as if I should go to bed at night unless I have made at least one new garment during the day."[2]

Janet and I talked about Mrs. Porter and the hard-working pioneer wives of her day, and we reached the obvious conclusion that, first of all, daughter Alyene pictured her mother at her best and not at her norm. "My life is certainly a far cry from hers, or vice versa," said Janet. "Can't you just see me sitting in a rocking chair shelling peas and quoting scriptures to a placid child at my knee?"

Janet's day is more one of telephones, car pools, forgotten appointments, juggled schedules and, as my mother would say, "meeting myself coming back."

A modern-day Mrs. Porter lives in Miami, Florida, and describes herself as a "reformed lousy housekeeper." Sandra Felton is founder of Messies Anonymous (5025 SW 114th Ave., Miami, Fla. 33165), an organization for training in housekeeping efficiency. How messy was Sandra Felton? So messy that she "would lose bills among all the accumulated stuff and have to root around looking for them before the electricity was shut off." She was so messy that rather than carting off old magazines to the trash can, she stacked them on any available surface until there were mounds of magazines. If she was faced with having guests for dinner, she was forced into a marathon cleaning frenzy.

How did Sandra become a cleanie? "There was no single day when she saw the light and became a neat housekeeper. There was no single incident that brought her to her knees—although the day she found the kitchen floor rotting because accumulated newspapers under the sink had gotten wet, came close."[3]

Janet and Sandra and other wives who feel confident about their housekeeping system suggest that you try, first of all, for periodic help: a cleaning woman (or man) as often as you can afford one, or a high school student. One wife prefers an all-day baby-sitter away from home so that she can be free to do heavy cleaning once or twice a month, with no children under foot. Several wives belong to baby-sitting pools, giving each mother a day or two a month for all-day cleaning, cooking, shopping or paying the bills.

A suggestion from Sandra is to start with one room and take about a month to clean, straighten and discard throughout the house. Pack rats have great difficulty in keeping a house clean, she says.

Housekeeping is not all a matter of appealing to the sense of sight, according to Janet. She thinks it's important to have luscious aromas coming from the oven and sexy fragrances coming from the bedroom. No doubt, God had the yukky smells in mind when he "thought of Noah and all the wild animals and the cattle with him in the ark." Psychologists tell us that the modern generation is sadly lacking in the solace and nostalgic bond-to-home that come from pleasant kitchen aromas. Mrs. J. Howard Williams, herself a minister's wife, told with pride of her daughter who rushed home after a busy day, barely arriving before her family did, and quickly put a piece of cinnamon toast in the oven to greet the nostrils of her hungry family. All of which makes me glad I'm a child of the generation that lived with aromas; the smell of sweet potatoes baking sends my mind's eye back to a warm kitchen on a cold day, just as watermelon conjures up visions of summer and the family together.

To keep a house clean takes time. To have "sweet smelling odor" erupting from the oven takes time. Newspapers and magazines abound with articles on how to use your time more effectively, how to find more hours in the day. And still it's up to you. The solution may be as simple as getting up thirty minutes early every morning or setting aside a day each month to make casseroles for the freezer. One wife, in her efforts to organize, got hooked on lists. She'd get up at 2:00 in the morning to make a schedule. Another similarly trapped wife had to give up on lists; she was becoming increasingly depressed as her list of things to do got longer each day instead of shorter. Yet, that would be my first suggestion to you: write it down. I could not function without a daily tally, without notes to myself from one end of the house to the other and without a family calendar by my telephone. I can relate to my friend's young granddaughter who had made herself a pre-school schedule, printed in her best first-grade lettering, the last entry being "wait." She explained that that was the last thing she did—*wait* for her car pool. Sounds like a good idea to me—a place on your list for waiting, for stopping, watching, smelling the roses.

If making lists is my first suggestion, my second one is to set priorities, weigh your family needs against your church's needs, or vice versa. A friend said to me that she was going around feeling very guilty about the fact that, instead of going to church on a certain Wednesday night, she had had her daughter's birthday dinner. Then she heard that the pastor's wife had missed prayer meeting to prepare a special meal for *her* daughter. "I felt better," she said. A pastor was involved in a much-needed, much-welcomed discussion with his teen-age son when it was time for a church meeting to begin, so he asked his wife to call in and let the chairman know he might not make it that evening. Just as your church comes first many days of the year, there will be times when it is necessary or expedient for you or your family to come first. Besides, your husband and your children need to know they are valuable in your line-up of concerns.

Even with priorities and organization intact, flexibility is the ingredient that gives sanity to routine. Gina said she used to go to bed at night enumerating the unfinished, untouched chores of the day, until she came to realize that the spur-of-the-moment happenings were just as valid as the planned ones. Also, as Louis and Kay Moore described their situation, "Just about the time we would get one system down pat, it seemed we were having to reshuffle it or abandon it in favor of another."[4]

Then all of us, unless we've finally learned better, waste time in playing the private investigator, attempting to name offenders and determine charges. Dr. Jack Orr says we have inherited a negative standard in this respect, "a view that it's important for families to fix blame. When something goes wrong, the first thing to do is to find out why the culprit acted as he or she did. All that energy goes into asking *why* and not *how* we can deal with the situation—how we can get beyond it, how we can get on with life and what we are trying to achieve together."[5]

Finally, I would say to you, don't procrastinate, don't spin your wheels. Whatever changes you need to make, now is the time. When our junior-high-schooler was reading a classic from "the olden days," he complained that the author had spent "a whole chapter just telling us what the guy looks like. I wish he'd get on with the story." Sometimes we need to skip the getting-ready-to-get-ready and get on with it.

It goes without saying that the more roles we play, the more likely it is that those roles will come in conflict with each other. The absent husband-father is a phenomenon of our times, so it behooves the wife-mother to learn to function in the dual role, or, literally, the quadrupled role. Jean Ford says that her husband is away from home about two-thirds of the time and that the good quality of their marriage and home life is due, pure and simple, to communication. Phone calls are on regular schedules, they and the children write letters back and forth, and when he is home, they talk in depth. "We find time alone is very important when he is gone so much. And because of his schedule, I have become an independent person and I'm glad I have. If something breaks around the house or goes wrong, I don't go to pieces. I know how to take care of the situation. The same is true with the car or with the children."[6]

That car is another phenomenon of our times. If I were starting over again, I'd take a course in automobile mechanics and I would get to know my service-station owner and garage mechanic as well as I know my doctor and dentist. One husband said he knows that when he returns home from his travels, part of his family's welcome can be attributed to the fact that a car or two needs his attention. A father of teen-agers says when he arrives home and sees the line-up of cars, he wonders which ones are not running today. You can perform a real service to yourself and to your family by being familiar with what's under the hood of your car.

"You really can become self-reliant," said Janet, "during these times when your husband is away. And that's not to be taken lightly, really. I have become quite knowledgeable as a plumber, electrician, gardener and general repairwoman. I am constantly amazed at how much money and time it saves me."

When the man of the family is absent a great deal of the time, that family learns to function without him. This may not be good for his ego, but it's bound to help keep him contented at home and away.

"It's handling the finances that gets me down," said Carol. "I hate paying bills, I can't balance a checkbook, I don't know a good buy from a bad one, I'm constantly in a panic about decisions I've made and I have this unrealistic feeling that the church people are looking over my shoulder." Many wives who do a good job of feeding the family, keeping the house in order and caring for emergencies are all thumbs when it comes to matters of money. If you said "me too" to Carol's frustrations, you need to sit down with your husband before the fact and work out some guidelines. Many couples actually attempt to live on their income without any semblance of a budget; this is courting disaster.

The church family probably wasn't looking over Carol's shoulder, but most likely the community was. Alice Taylor said that when she attended a private school where girls wore uniforms, they were told that, while in such dress, everything they did reflected on the school. I feel the same way when I drive a car bearing a school sticker on the window. I know that if I'm an unfriendly driver, the person behind me gets a negative picture of the school. So it is with you as a minister's wife; you represent the church. If your credit rating is bad, creditors may say, "Church people don't pay their bills." If you and your husband are not above reproach in your financial ethics, people will wonder why the church isn't keeping you in line.

On the questionnaire, I asked, "Do you consider ministers' salaries adequate?" Fifty-nine said "yes" and fifty-one said "no." During these days, any family with an "adequate" income is most fortunate. If, however, you're with the ladies in the fifty-one group, you may have to help add to the family wages.

If you want to remain at home with your part-time (or full-time) job, the opportunities are there, depending, of course, on the size and needs of your town. You can teach piano lessons or tutor students from first grade up. You can make and sell arts and crafts or baked goods. I have several friends who have opened their own shops, having developed these talents and dreams while staying at home raising children. Every fall I receive invitations to numerous holiday bazaars where young mothers combine their year-long efforts and make their own Christmas money. And, if you haven't tried it, you'd be surprised at the benefits of an annual garage sale.

Put your secretarial skills to good use at home: typing, bookkeeping, proofreading, etc. Our daughter Beth uses her Spanish at home to translate reports and contracts for businesses. A seamstress I know specializes in making holiday and party costumes only; she has a booming business.

If none of these ideas is feasible for you, your chances for work away from home that will fit into your schedule are still worth pursuing. Employers in all businesses and professions are finding it necessary to consider the value of part-time workers in order to obtain the skills they need and, at the same time, accommodate parents with school-age children.

Of course, you need to keep in mind that with employment away from home, vacation days are rare and you will be limited in such luxuries as being able to travel with your husband, being at home with house guests or staying with a sick child. A survey of school-teachers revealed that one of the major attractions of their profession is time off in the summer and at Christmas.

Still, it comes down to your theories about money versus your real needs. Being as poor as a church mouse is not the difficulty for some people that it is for others. Gina touched upon a problem that we seldom think of when we consider ministers and their salaries. Her two brothers are successful professional men who make a great deal more money than Gina's husband does. "The first thing I had to grapple with," said Gina, "was the injustice of it all. My husband went to school just as long as my brothers did; he's just as much a professional in his field as they are in theirs. And yet his income is like half of theirs. Mind you, I, not my husband, was having trouble with this. Frank made his decision to be a minister with his eyes wide open; this realization was my final salvation in accepting our financial situation. The next thing I had to settle with myself was that our lifestyle is going to be different from that of my brothers and their families. Our house is smaller, our luxuries are fewer. We can't go on expensive trips with them or send our children to the same summer camps. But through the years my feelings have been more than salved by seeing how much my nieces and nephews enjoy visiting us, how my sisters-in-law call me for advice and by the great, relaxed fun we have when we all get together."

So, first of all, you must settle in your own mind what Gina called her "sin of materialism." Think of all the sermons you've heard on "the root of all kinds of evil" and "where your treasure is your heart is" and vice versa, and remind yourself that those ideas really are true, because they are; then give some monetary value to good health, friendships, a good marriage, the love of God—and you'll come up rich.

Moses, in one of his cooking lessons to his people, said, "Bake what you want to bake, and boil what you want to boil," which, if we bring it down to modern terms, means the kitchen is yours and the meals are yours and therein may lie the dilemma. Family meals, unfortunately, have lost some of their formality and, in some cases, even their existence. My father-in-law, who for all of his seventy-plus years had been a man of traditional Christian breakfasts with the saying of grace and reading of scriptures and the family all together, was visiting us during a typical school and work week. He was the first person in for breakfast, seating himself in anticipation of a good hot meal and family fellowship. Vernon, running late for the office, grabbed a glass of juice and took off, his father still seated, waiting. One by one, our three high-schoolers partook of what one might loosely call breakfast, rushing and gulping, each rising from the table to leave an amazed grandfather at his place still. Finally, when the door slammed for the last time, there sat the waiting patriarch, still unfed, still disbelieving! Which was typical of the breakfasts he and I shared during those years.

I would like to think that you can do better than that, that your household is so well organized and your husband and children so attuned to the beauties and decorum of the mornings that your breakfasts will be all you've dreamed they'll be. If, on the other hand, you are bondwoman to crying babies, car pools, football practice and frenzied family departures, you may find that your best time of the day is when you succumb to that blessed after-breakfast quiet and eat, pray and meditate alone.

In spite of all the obstacles to calm family meals, they still remain our best prospects for togetherness. If you have only two or three times during the entire week when the family is complete, make it special—not just the food and the setting, but, more importantly, the conversation. Or if you feel that the three-times-a-day everyday is a real drag, you need to make some changes. Recently I listened to a prominent chef who was attempting to justify his premise that men are better cooks than women. His reasoning was that women are more "structured" in their cooking, whereas men are more adventurous. "Men have more fun," he said. "Women feel they must be right and this cramps their style." So break out and use your imagination.

Make birthdays and anniversaries special. Have a favorite meal or favorite dish to celebrate accomplishments. Your husband may not make it to all these; he may not even be there when he's the honored one, but, from time to time, it will be just as you have planned.

Don't let meals or dirty floors or any other form of housekeeping prevent you from going with your husband or child to ball games or school programs or anywhere else. Take it from those of us who've been there, Little League really doesn't last forever and all the recitals and parent-teacher meetings will soon be a thing of the past. There will even be a time when it won't be so earthshaking if your husband doesn't come home for dinner; you can be where he is. And I know what you're thinking. When I had three babies and was up to my chin in diapers and bottles and my fondest dream was a night's sleep, well-wishers reminded me that these were the best days of my life and I wondered what on earth it must be like on down the road! But it does pass, so don't postpone this gratification.

You may need to change some routines, if for no other reason than to wake up the people who live in your house. Just as moving furniture around gets attention, a flip-flop in your humdrum life will do it too. Picture the mother who meets her children at the door after school to announce that she and Daddy have sold the TV and replaced it with games and books! I knew one such mother. Or take the father who comes home with seeds and shovel and says, "From now on we raise our vegetables." One Labor Day we decided to observe the day according to its name: laboring. The seven of us—father, mother, and five children ages five to seventeen—spent the day getting our yard in shape. Of course, there was vying for being the indoors telephone-answerer, and more than one person offered to do the dishes or clean rooms that day. But when the exhausted crew finished, one five-year-old sighed, grinned and announced that "this is the first time I ever sweated under my arms."

Take off some Saturday and spend the day at a place where you've never been: a state park, a historic shrine, a drive through farm lands. If you have a small child too young to appreciate such excursions, get a sitter for him for that day. Invite people over for hamburgers; do it on the spur of the moment, change the routine.

Joseph Bayly of David C. Cook Publishing Company wrote, in a testament to his children, "I believe my generation's greatest loss—next to the inviolateness of marriage and the family—has been the sanctity of the Lord's Day....I hope you will try to recapture it as a retreat from the world; try to turn it into the happiest day of the week."[7]

Gerald Nachman of the *Chicago Tribune* put it another way: "Back in the old days, Sunday had character. It was prim, but underneath it had a certain toughness, some confidence and a sense of security. It was the most sturdy and unflappable of days, one people could count on; there was structure to it."[8]

If you can capture—or recapture—that, you've brought a bit of magic to your family and yourself. Such Sundays are hard to come by these days, but we are told that "the Lord has *given* you the Sabbath," which makes it a special day. Janie says, "Be sure you're prayed up on Sundays"—the day goes better. Janet explained that the seasoned minister's wife knows Sunday *has* to be a day of rest for her husband as much as is possible. She needs to guard the door and the telephone so that he can rest during the afternoon, especially if he is responsible for another service that night. Hopefully, in the process, you too can sit down and put your feet up and read the paper. Hopefully also, the church people know you are resting because you have made this clear to them.

My husband reminisces often about the Sundays of his boyhood: like knowing by the look on his mother's face as she sat in the choir that he should go home (which usually was next door) and check on the roast, or retrieving the family dog who had a habit of coming to church just as the sermon started. But he, like other children of ministers with whom I've talked, has emerged with a reverence for the day.

And, like other pastors' sons and daughters, he profited from those who were guests in the home, whether it was for Sunday dinner or for the week-long revival. You too will look back on these times as some of the best things that happened to you and your family. One son, now a college professor, said his interest in history began as he listened to a missionary who spent a week in his home. Ruth Porter learned the fine points of being a hostess as she helped her mother entertain in the parsonage. "But there is always the possibility," said Ruth, "that the pastor's wife is so busy entertaining the church family or staff members or out-of-town guests that she neglects her own children and their friends. This happened to me when I was a child. Very seldom did I sit at a dinner table with anyone my age. So I have been very careful about that with my children; they've been free to invite their friends even when we had special dinner guests."

Then there were the minister and his wife who sent their two children to stay with friends during a revival meeting in order to make room in their own house and at their table for the visiting evangelist and singer!

Ruth says one of the greatest advances in ministry wifehood is the demise of the parsonage. "Now that most of us are free to choose our own place to live, we avoid some of the headaches of my mother's day—the big one being lack of privacy. Our house was used more like a church annex than a home. Daddy put a lock on my bedroom door so that at times when activity was going on at the church, I could study or dress without having people barging into my room."

"We may not have the parsonage," said Denise, "but we still have the telephone. I have a minister's-wife friend who actually went to work to avoid the phone—and she had *wanted* to be a stay-at-home mother. And the other day I heard of a wife who arranged for an office at the church for her hideaway." The wife of a pastor of a large city church had an answering service installed. Now she spends an hour or so a day returning calls. This has met with disfavor among some church members, but it is her solution to what she considered a major problem.

Ruth Truman has another suggestion: "Know your husband's secretary well. Let her know how you feel about being disturbed at home by phone. Clue her in when you or the kids are sick. Let her be your partner in crime at snatching a private day or two away from the parish."[9]

Besides, his secretary can get messages from you to him and hopefully can get some answers from him to you. This line of communication is a great asset for you, so cultivate the relationship. I've observed some marvelous friendships between wives and secretaries.

Jean Reynolds Davis's husband didn't have a secretary when they were in their first pastorate. Jean found out on a Friday afternoon that she was pregnant. When she got home from the doctor's office, her husband was out on church business. He called about 8:00 to say he would be home late, not to wait up for him. She could have told him then, she said, but hers seemed the sort of message one didn't tell the expectant father by phone. Saturday went as Friday had gone—no time for the big announcement. So on Sunday morning she took a card from the pew rack and filled it out, checking the part that said, "would like Rector to call" and placed it in the offering plate. Sure enough, the Rector called and the Rector's wife got her private audience!

If Jean Reynolds Davis can find a way, so can you. Mrs. Landrum Leavell said to seminary wives, "Don't postpone happiness. You can be just as happy right where you are, struggling, as you'll be ten years from now. You don't just suddenly get happy when you get all the things you want."[10] Harold Kushner said it in different words: "Can you forgive the world's imperfections and love it because it is capable of containing great beauty and because it is the only world we have?"[11] For the same reasons, can you not love *your* small world, your place, your house because it is your portion? Paul wrote to Timothy, "Godliness with contentment is great gain." Make that into a sampler and hang it on your kitchen wall.

> As the marsh hen secretly builds
> on the watery sod,
> Behold, I will build me a nest
> on the greatness of God.
> —Sidney Lanier

Your home is *yours*, and it's up to you to decide what goes on inside your four walls.

NOTES

1. Terry Hekker, *Ever Since Adam and Eve* (New York: Wm. Morrow and Co., 1979), p. 49.
2. Alyene Porter, *Papa Was A Preacher* (Old Tappan, NJ: Fleming H. Revell Co., Spire Books, 1972), p. 100.
3. Linda Cicero, "Can't Find the Floor Because of the Dirt? Join the Messy Crowd," *Houston Post*, May 18, 1981, p. 4B.
4. Louis and Kay Moore, *When You Both Go to Work* (Waco, TX: Word Books, 1982), p. 148.

5. Dr. Jack Orr, "Families: The Paradox of Perfection," Wilmington, DE, 1981, p. 5.

6. Jean Ford, "A Visit with Jean Ford," *Family Life Today*, Jan. 1981, p. 7.

7. Joseph Bayly, "A Father's Testament to His Children," *Family Life Today*, Jan. 1981, p. 11.

8. Gerald Nachman, "The Lost Weekend," *Reader's Digest*, Oct. 1981, p. 138.

9. Ruth Truman, *Underground Manual for Ministers' Wives* (Nashville: Abingdon, 1974), p. 73.

10. Martha Nelson, *This Call We Share* (Nashville: Broadman, 1977), p. 137.

11. Harold Kushner, *When Bad Things Happen to Good People* (New York: Schocken Books, 1981), p. 148.

PKs

The title of this chapter is really a misnomer. Not all ministers are preachers. Therefore your child, rather than being a PK, a Preacher's Kid, may be a Music Minister's Kid or a Minister of Education's Kid. So whether PK, MMK, MEK, or any other K, raising children in your stained glass house is not easy. Raising children in any house is not easy.

A first-grader made a great discovery: "MOM" upside down is "WOW"! Even upside-down MOM is WOW. Which is good, because often Mom, in spite of her design to be the perfect Mom, will be upside down. And inside-out and head-over-heels and every other physical and emotional contortion that comes to mind.

But hear this: a recent study shows that Mom—not Dad, not the dog—is man's best friend. A survey of young men and adolescent boys revealed that sons feel most comfortable talking with mothers about dating, sex, manners, school, friendships, pressures, emotions, feelings, privacy and entertainment![1]

However, such studies tend to point out one of the distresses of our times—too much mothering and too little fathering. So your better part of wisdom may be to work on that too little fathering bit. Use whatever honorable wiles you have at hand to bring Dad into your child's life, assuming, of course, that Dad's the less-participating parent in your family. Our world is in dire need of a generation more influenced by fathers, grandfathers and uncles.

One PK, as a teen-ager, was having trouble accepting her role as daughter of the church pastor. "Then one day," she said, "I sat myself down and asked myself, 'Do you like having your father for a father?' and I answered myself, 'Yes, I do.' Then I decided I could tolerate being a Preacher's Kid in order to have this special man as my dad."

But back to Mom. Assuming that you've started your child's life off with a great deal of prayer and concern and knowing that you love him, *relax*. Uptight mothers breed uptight children. John Drescher said that if he were starting his family over again, he'd laugh more *with* his children. He quotes Charles Buxton: "The first duty to children is to make them happy. If you have not made them so, you have wronged them."[2] Ruth Porter says "amen" to that. She was brought up prim and proper in a pastor's home and no one laughed much. "Even as an adult, it was difficult for me to think of laughter as more than poking fun. Fortunately, I married a man with a sense of humor (God was watching out for me, for sure!), and our house is full of laughter."

Of course, you have to watch your words because you may have to eat them and because they set an example for your children. We had at our house what we called school-bus words. If you asked, "Where did you hear that word?" the answer came back, "Oh, that's a bus word." So your child will pick them up without any help from you, but, without reinforcement, most of them will fall by the wayside.

Keeping up with the Joneses is a futile game played by many clergy mothers. Ruth Senter confirms this with her most memorable experience in doing someone else's thing. It was a cold Wisconsin February and she had decided not to take her nine-month-old baby and older child and go on the winter retreat for which her husband was speaker. However, when she learned that the wife of another speaker, whose baby was even younger than nine months, was going, she "bundled everyone up and we headed north to the cold woods. It took our family four weeks to get over that retreat. We went from infection to infection....One of the things I said to myself during that time was that it didn't matter how anyone else did it; what mattered was how the Senter family did it."[3]

You really do have to do your own thinking. A friend of mine said that when she was a young mother and minister's wife, she was criticized by some for being at home too much and by others for being at the church too much.

Then, of course, other people are going to be caring for and influencing your children, and this is good—usually. One expert in the field of child care revealed his speculation that eventually most children will be raised by someone other than their parents. If your children are close to their grandparents, they are among the blessed. Author Terry Hekker says grandparents offer more affection "than a pony and more security than five trust accounts." The extended family is a need of our times; children learn great life lessons from grandparents.

Don't discount the part in your child's life played by school teachers, coaches and baby-sitters. One of my newlywed class members was fraught with great fear over the prospect of becoming a mother. "What if I don't raise our child right? What if he or she becomes a criminal or doesn't turn out to be a good person?" She was oblivious to the fact that others, God and Daddy and those in between, would be involved in molding this child's character; she was assuming too much responsibility.

One of the crimes being imposed on our children is the use of TV as a baby-sitter. Our family speaks often of our TV repairman who hated TV. All the time he was working with the tubes and wires at the back of our TV set, he spoke with vehemence of the families in our neighborhood who "couldn't live without their TVs," those who let their children watch it from morning till night and, worst of all, those who leave small children alone at home with the TV as a baby-sitter. Walter Cronkite, speaking of the misuse and overuse of TV in America, said, "All books are not classics, all magazines are not good; why do we expect all TV to be good?" Grandparents are better than TV, for sure, and people are better than things; your children deserve the better.

There seems to be no end to our society's batting back and forth of the expression "quality time"—what it is, how much it is, how to recognize it, how to use it. Psychologist Lee Salk says that "when someone asks me about quality versus quantity, they're asking for permission to do less."[4] Heidi Heard, who was periodically a discussion leader in my marriage and parenting class, is a talented and busy mother of one and step-mother of four. "I'm a feminist," she told my class, "but they've fed us a bill of goods on quality time. What children need is quality time 24 hours a day." Actually, what our children need is quality time in quantity; maybe there should be fewer discourses about either-or.

Jonja Deal, an MK (Missionary's Kid), was in school in the United States; her parents were at their mission post in Jordan. Someone had given Jonja a gift of an eight-minute phone call to her folks. She wanted to make sure her parents could talk to her from a good phone, so arrangements were made days in advance and the parents had to make a one-and-a-half hour trip to a missionary apartment complex in order to be sure of a good connection. Jonja said she wanted to be sure that the eight minutes were quality time!

Strickland Gillian was speaking of quality time when he wrote

> You may have tangible wealth untold,
>   Caskets of jewels and coffers of gold.
> Richer than I you never can be;
>   I had a mother who read to me.[5]

Sadly, many ministers' children have too many parents, too many overseers. Ruth says no preacher's child can ever feel that he or she is "incognito." She says that even now, as a mature wife and mother, she can go into a church hundreds of miles from home and "feel this burning behind my ears that whispers 'Look, there's the preacher's daughter.'"

After the death of his daughter Carole, L. D. Johnson found among her high school papers notes she had used in a speech about being a preacher's daughter:

"All PKs are divided into one of two categories by outsiders. We are either very saintly or else we are worse than other people. There doesn't seem to be an average preacher's kid. Of the two extremes, I don't know which I prefer."

Later she touched on the saintly image. "Have you ever had the experience of coming upon a group in conversation and having them stop in embarrassed silence because they didn't want you to hear what they were talking about? When this happens to me, I feel like shouting, 'I'm human, too. I eat; I brush my hair; I cry; I go to school; and I even enjoy a good joke! Or as Shylock puts it, 'If you prick us, do we not bleed? If you tickle us, do we not laugh?'"[6]

One mother started very early trying to avoid the PK syndrome. She says she does not tell her young son that Daddy has gone to church; she tells him Daddy has gone to work. Then on Wednesdays and Sundays they "go to church."

My friend Helen says she would raise her child differently; she would not *make* her go to church. "So often, she knew it was for the benefit of her parents' image and not for her. That's not a good reason to go to church."

As my daughter watched a TV sitcom some time back, I wondered how she would feel, watching that particular episode, if her father were a minister. On the show, a pastor went to the psychologist for help. When the secretary learned he was a clergyman, she covered her legs with her skirt, and apologized for her humor. Of course, sport is made of lawyers and teachers and men of all professions, but somehow, it seems less weighty in the secular vein. The minister's child lives under an ever-present badge of identity.

Yet you can't undo that. In spite of whatever disadvantages your child may have as a PK, there are equally as many pluses. You will be smart to major on those.

Even by osmosis they learn. My friend Lois and her five-year-old granddaughter, Jennifer, were having lunch at the fried chicken restaurant. They took their plates and sat down at a table. Jennifer looked at her grandmother and said, "Let's say the blessing, but let's say it to ourselves." She paused, then added, "And let's say it with our eyes open." Even so, she had learned that eating food is a time for thanking God.

Emily Kimbrough tells of another five-year-old who knew about the ritual of saying grace at meals. Little Alida was spending the night with cousins in another city. She "felt uneasy as a visitor, but lifting her head after silent grace, with a deep sigh of contentment, she said, 'This is just like home. We smell our plates too.'"[7]

Jean Ford says their family tries not to dwell on negatives and failure, that even though one can learn from looking back and from checking off the uglies, it's better to live in the present and look to the future. "Leighton and I are certainly not anywhere near perfect. We make many mistakes and we sin and fall and stumble...but I hope we are able to admit our mistakes and confess our sins to each other and to our children."[8]

Which is a far cry from other situations described to me by sons and daughters of ministers, ones who say their parents never admitted wrongdoing, never said, "I'm sorry" and, according to one daughter, "My father always left the impression that whatever he did was approved of God—and the same type of misdeed on my part was disapproved by God."

You will receive a lot of reports on your child's behavior. Most of these will be tucked away in what a casual observer would hear as an innocent comment but which you know is a loaded accusation. Like "I understand the Youth Director really had problems with the boys at camp last week" or "Isn't it sad the way our girls misbehave in church on Sunday nights?" Experienced mothers say don't pick up on it and don't go home and give your child the third degree. Do talk about church and do talk about the Youth Camp; you'll know if there's a problem. After all, guilt needs no accuser.

"Preachers' kids have to learn to throw dirt clods instead of rocks," says David Smith. "Breaking windows, denting cars, hitting the side of a house and hurting people are all worse if done with a rock instead of a clod...and if done by a PK." He said his dad's sermon to him about rock-throwing went like this: "Don't throw rocks. But if you just have to throw something, throw a ball. Be careful doing that. Don't hit anyone. And when you throw at Treece's chickens in our garden, throw dirt clods—small ones."[9]

One of the nicest boys we ever had in our home was our son's friend Kent. And yet on frequent Sunday mornings Kent could be seen sitting in the hall in the pseudo pre-school dunce chair, often with *our* son, and almost always with *some*one's son. As part of the "fearsome foursome" of the elementary area, his name was often tossed about, mostly because he was a minister's son and because he was expected by many to behave as an adult.

"But," said Janet, "when you write about ministers' children, don't make it sound like we think they should be allowed to run wild and no one in the church should lift an eyebrow. After all, I get upset with other people's children sometimes; I certainly understand when they get upset with mine. I just don't want them to expect more of the pastor's children than they do of other children."

Then Janet said something I hadn't heard from other mothers. "Is it so unreasonable, though, that people should expect me and my children to be examples of good Christians? After all, we are a Christian family; people need a pattern. And if the pastor's family isn't it, where is it coming from?"

Often it's the parent who expects unwarranted behavior from the child, and that, according to experts, leaves more scars than the disapproval of outsiders.

A young visiting minister was preaching "in view of a call." A woman of the church noticed that the young wife, sitting near her, was very, very nervous all during the service. When it ended, she took the young woman's hand and said, "It's all right, it's going to be okay." And the wife said, "I'm so worried about my children in the nursery, that they'll misbehave." We are mistaken when we consider the quiet, unmoving child as the well-behaved one.

Parents often measure children by what other children their age are doing. This is true from the toddler who doesn't walk at ten months to the teen-ager who isn't dating yet. We have late bloomers in our family. During the Christmas holidays when our son Jon was in junior high and in love with basketball, his friend Kent was coming from out of town for a visit in our city. Four sneaky girl-type junior-high-schoolers planned a party at Gordon's house for themselves and the Fearsome Foursome of yesteryear. I was standing in the kitchen near the phone when Jon got the call from Carlyn inviting him to the party. He said, "I'll call you back." Then he made a call of his own, "Gordon, do you have a light over your basketball goal?" A second for the positive answer, then a call back to Carlyn, "Yes, I can come."

Each child is unique; children need to develop at their own speed. Jon finally gave up basketballs—though not completely—for girls, then narrowed the field down to one girl to marry.

If the average child is overprogrammed—as is often the case—and spends too little time alone, thinking, dreaming and doing his or her own thing, this is even more common with ministers' children. They are likely to be deluged with invitations, with meeting new people, with opportunities to join organizations and take lessons. You may have to protect them from overextending themselves and see that they have some unstructured time. We have friends who have two daughters; one was a "joiner," one was not. Both grew into beautiful womanhood and even though their lifestyles are still different, each is functioning as a well-adjusted, happy wife and mother.

On the questionnaire to ministers' wives I asked, "Do you think your child's behavior influences (or did influence) your husband's effectiveness as a minister?" Only twenty-five said "No." One said, "Does it ever!" Among those who thought the child's behavior *was* influential, most felt the father had been helped by his child. One wife said, "My husband says he was never able to preach with feeling about problems of parents and children until he himself was a parent." And another wrote, "Our children are my husband's panacea."

I discussed this question with Ellen Jones. She agreed that often too much emphasis is given to the day-by-day conduct of the minister's children. "After all," she said, "most young people are less than enchanted by adults and they often are preoccupied with their own world; they are more concerned with the moment, with impressing their peers, and they are basically shy."

Often you will find it difficult to explain things to your child without condemning someone in the church or without letting your anger show. Sometimes you'll have to explain that even though other children do certain things, yours may not, that it might even be right for other children but not right for yours. We lay mothers deal in the same differentials; the challenge seems to be endless.

And then you try so hard to drive home a point, to make with the never-to-be-forgotten discourse, and it lands with a thud on tender ears. Our station wagon was making its way to church one sunny Sunday spring morning, its seven passengers spic and span in their righteous robes, when what passes in front of us but another automobile pulling a sleek new boat headed toward the waters. Someone from the back seat surmised, "I'll bet they're going to Galveston." I felt that that was my shining moment, my God-given opening to sermonize to my envious, earth-bound brood. "They really should be going to church, shouldn't they?" I said. But I hadn't reckoned with the interpretation that I should have known would come from our four-year-old Richard the literalist, sitting in the left corner. "There's no water at the church," he said.

Becoming a teen-ager is not easy. Becoming the parent of a teen-ager is not easy. Tallulah Bankhead was visiting friends who had a particularly obnoxious teen-age son. "We just don't know what to make of him," confessed the mother. Tallulah suggested, "How about a rug?"

A common temptation.

Dean Acheson, in his book *Morning and Noon*, wrote of this time in his life: "If I had known then that adolescence is more often than not a disturbed time, when unhappiness and joy are most unevenly measured out, it would have brought proportion to my thoughts."[10]

Thomas Jefferson, in response to a question from John Adams about living his life over again, said, "From age twenty-five to sixty, yes, but no lower down."

The load is heavy when the rebellious child becomes a rebellious adult. And, unhappily, this sequence takes place in ministers' families just as it does in other families. At that point, there is little help in looking back and searching the "whys." But those who have suffered and are suffering because of grown-up children now lost to drugs, alcohol and the many forms of corruptions have hearts and heads full of advice for you:

1. First of all, be sure they know you accept them as the y are and that you don't wish they were like someone else.
2. Set limits; there is security in knowing where the line is drawn.
3. Show your approval of them.
4. Go a step further; tell them you love them.
5. Show genuine interest in what they are doing; they can tell if you're not concerned.
6. Communicate. Which includes listening.
7. Be civil to their friends, even if you don't like them.
8. Laugh with them. Life shouldn't always be serious.

9. Don't accuse them of lying—or of doing anything else you aren't *sure* they did.
10. Give them undivided, unpreoccupied time; that's what they want most from you.

My brother Mike, the youngest of seven children, was overheard saying to college friends, "I cannot recall a single moment in my life when I did not feel loved." One wise mother said, "If my children are going to have problems from either too much love or too little love, I'd certainly prefer it be from too *much.*"

I was visiting my brother George in his hospital room. He had received mail from his grandchildren. The one from nine-year-old Isaac ended with, "I love you, Granddad." George explained that those words from Isaac were a real breakthrough. "Isaac has had trouble saying 'I love you,'" said George, "but he and I have been working on it. I've been reminding him often of my love for him by saying, 'I love you, Isaac,' and now he can say, 'I love you, Granddad.'"

Let's pick up on number ten in our list, the one about unpreoccupied time. Just as the small child often holds mother's face in her hands and says "Look at me," the older child many times wishes to do the same thing. Louis McBurney says many clergy parents consciously or unconsciously sacrifice their children on "the altar of service to the church, or to the expectations of the community. When you are too busy to know him, too distracted to listen, or too self-centered to show interest and give him approval, the sacrifice is made."[11]

One minister who had gone through a divorce and whose children had caused grief to him and his wife said, "It was so easy for us to blame the church—for our divorce, for our children's problems, for the whole blessed mess. But other families survive church life: I see beautiful adults who were raised in ministers' homes, I see great marriages. So the finger has to be pointed at me; I can't go on blaming the church."

What surfaces in your young child as a strong spirit or an iron will can be channeled, and he will benefit from having been a spirited beginner molded into a wholesome adult. Within your guidelines, he must have room for that.

I was sitting in the chapel at Mrs. O'Neil's funeral service. Mrs. O'Neil had been a beloved keeper of babies at our church for many years. The organist played "Jesus Loves Me" and "Praise Him, Praise Him," and the preacher stood to deliver the eulogy for the memorial service. For the entire time he was speaking, an infant in his mother's arms at the back of the chapel alternated between whimpering and gurgling. I kept wondering why the mother didn't take him out, why she would let him disturb the service like that. I was duly condemned when the preacher concluded his message with "—and isn't it appropriate that one of her little ones should be here this morning making happy sounds?"

When your child has disappointments, he will hurt, and so will you. It's what author Jess Lair calls "your pain in my heart." The anguish grows as the child grows; he shakes it off more easily when he's young.

Toughing it out is often as hard on parents as it is on the child. And there are times when parents need help. One pastor tells of meeting a couple at a retreat who wanted to talk. Their son had had three broken marriages, their daughter had died of cancer. The three of them talked for hours; the parents needed help. A friend who likes being a pastor's wife and who says she has had a minimum of problems still believes that all members of ministers' families should have access to professional counseling, "if for no other reason than to have an unbiased person to talk to."

Expect some trauma when you uproot your child at any age after infancy and move to another church. And when she doesn't make the drill team or he gets cut from the football squad, don't say, "Oh, it's all right," or, "That's not so bad." It isn't all right and it is bad. Empathy is needed; "I know it hurts" is your line.

Then there's the turning loose, the letting go. If someone should ask me to name a difficult time in my parenthood, off the top of my head, I'd say it was the time I watched each one go off in a car alone, just after getting a driver's license. But then a friend said it's even worse to see them get in a car with someone else who just got a driver's license!

A student wrote an editorial for his college paper about breaking away from his father, now that he's a university man. He started by saying, "I'm not so sure trying to be like ole Dad is so important. It seems to be happening without a whole lot of effort on my part. And frankly, I find it kind of scary." Then he ended with "It's certainly not disrespectful to acknowledge that your parents aren't perfect and they may have passed on some tendencies you'll want to discard. We've got to learn from their mistakes as well as from their victories. I still enjoy the thought of being a lot like my father, but I surely am glad I do have some choice in the matter."[12]

That's breaking away with finesse.

One mother said she learned by the mistakes she made with her first child and attempted to improve with the next child. Instead of saying to her teen-ager, "You can't do this" and "You must do that," she says, "You can smoke and get cancer or you can quit and save your health. You can go to college and earn a living with your head or you can continue as you are and work with your back." The choice is his, and his parents have learned to release themselves from the responsibility of his decisions.

Those in authority tell us that you help your child to become a self-sufficient, responsible adult by *encouraging* him into it. If he writes a good school paper, take note of it. If he looks nice when he's dressed to go out, compliment him. If he tries and fails, don't condemn him. If you don't know the answer, ask *him*—even if you think he doesn't know it. And when he does something for you, say "Thank you."

During his son Scot's preschool years Spencer Moore spent his day off each week with him. They might go by his office to take care of an emergency or they might go to the zoo. But all day long father and son were together; it was bound to have made an impact.

Sometimes it's easier to turn loose than you think it will be. Vernon had made plans to spend the evening at home with our sons, having dinner and watching Monday night football. As he walked in the front door, they walked out the back—on their way to watch the game with their friend Bill. And Vernon spent the evening alone.

Our daughter Beth made for me a wall hanging which I lovingly placed in our den. It reads: "There are only two lasting things we can leave our children: one is roots and the other is wings."

As your child is learning to pitch his own tent and spread his own wings, he is gaining some special insights that will hold him in good stead by the simple fact that he is a PK. How so?

First of all, he learns to care about people because you and your husband are in the business of caring about people. I see this characteristic time and time again in adults and young people who grew up in ministers' homes. I see it in my own husband who observes people's needs long before I do and has a special sense of what to do about them.

Your child will learn to weather the storm, for he has seen you survive and he has heard about members of the congregation who have been through the valleys. He will be at ease among people and, hopefully, he will have learned the fine art of communication. And because his father probably supported the family on a modest income, he will learn frugality. Brace yourself for a fantastic adult!

Author David Smith said he developed his concept of God by observing and listening to older people, many people in many towns and churches and at many meals in his home.

Minette Drumwright, both the daughter and wife of a minister, looks back on family devotions as a very sustaining and growing part of her life and the lives of her husband and her children. Janie, also the daughter and wife of a minister, gives credit to her parents for the fact that she is confident in her role as a minister's wife. And Ruth, in spite of the fact that her childhood was lived out in a strait-laced environment, says, "My inner braces are intact and for that I am most grateful."

If you've raised up your child in the way he should go, if you've claimed the promises, and still, as a teen-ager, a college student, a young adult, he turns his back on your teachings and chooses a way of life apart from the church, your situation is not as unique as you may think. Time after time, as I talked with mothers, I heard the desperate cry for the child who lives his life outside the church arena. One devoted mother, wife of a prominent pastor, said, "I can't fault anyone or anyone's children; I have three children and four grandchildren and not a one of them ever goes to church."

Another mother, really more concerned about her grandchildren's lack of religious training than about her daughter's indifference, happened upon a plan that she hoped would work—for at least *one* Sunday. During the week before Mother's Day, she called her daughter and suggested that, in honor of the day, the six of them—children, parents and grandparents—might go to church together, then out to a special restaurant for dinner. The daughter said she'd check with her husband and call back. The next day she called her mother and said, "We've talked about it and what we'd like to do is skip the church part but meet you for dinner." Quick as a flash came the mother's reply, "Sorry. It's a package deal."

A New York taxi driver told us that one of his passengers from the day before was a well-known businessman who, speaking of his children, said, "I have five kids and not a star in the bunch." And who is a star? The son who is the clone of his father? The daughter who marries well? After all, the daffodil doesn't become a flower overnight; a man's worth is not measured by another man's deeds. My brother Harry often quoted Thomas Jefferson, mostly because he just liked to quote Jefferson, but also because this one particular Jefferson quote found kinship in Harry's life: "My father was a farmer so I could be a scientist so my children could be artists." Stars in all three generations.

Of the people listed in *Who's Who in America*, more are sons and daughters of ministers than of fathers in any other profession. Our questionnaire reveals that almost a third of the ministers on our list are sons of ministers. Our church attempted to compile a list of PKs and MKs among our membership to have a special dinner in their honor; we were amazed at the large number of ministers' sons and daughters working in our church.

Two testimonials from PKs typify the many I have read:

Peter John Marshall: "By the time I finished college, my rebellion had soared. It was at this time I realized my youthful cynicism was not the fault of my parents, or the society of which I was a part, but solely a result of my refusal to accept the love of Christ and God's plan for my life. The seeds planted in me by my parents' faith had begun to sprout."[13]

Leon Jaworski: "Several people have inspired me, but from the standpoint of morals and ethics, I would have to say my father. He was a minister of the gospel. Just growing up loving him helped shape me."[14]

"The offspring of the righteous shall be delivered." "Raise up a child in the way he should go and when he is old, he will not depart from it." These promises sustain me daily.

Guy Greenfield, in his book *The Wounded Parent*, says it takes months and sometimes years to see the fruition take place and that impatient parents can impede the outcome. "God has a way of working wonders if we will give Him the room and the time to do it His way. For most modern parents, patience comes hard. We have a low tolerance for pain. We want instant relief."[15]

Your adventure in mothering is just that, an adventure, which the dictionary defines as "a hazardous or exciting experience, a daring feat." And don't forget the Heavenly Cycle: "As a mother comforts her child, so will I myself comfort you" (Isa. 66:13).

Your PK is PS, Pretty Special. In no time at all you'll be sitting in your empty nest, wondering where the years went.

NOTES

1. Nat Brandt, ed., ABC-TV staff, "Who's A Boy's Best Buddy?" *Family Circle*, Nov. 16, 1982, p. 70.
2. John Drescher, *If I Were Starting My Family Again* (Nashville: Abingdon, 1979), p. 18.
3. Ruth Senter, *So You're the Pastor's Wife* (Grand Rapids, MI: Zondervan, 1979), p. 26.
4. Joe A. Cox and Kris Moore, *The Impact of Children and the Dual-Career Family* (Waco, TX: Baylor University Press, 1981), p. 4.
5. Strickland Gillian, "The Reading Mother," *The Book of Life* (Chicago: John Rudin & Co., 1948), Introduction.
6. L. D. Johnson, *The Morning after Death* (Nashville: Broadman Press, 1978), p. 32.
7. Emily Kimbrough, *Now and Then* (New York: Harper & Row, 1972), p. 104.
8. Jean Ford, "A Visit With Jean Ford," *Family Life Today*, Jan. 1981, p. 29.
9. David Smith, *Remember the Good Times* (Nashville: Broadman, 1978), p. 48.
10. Dean Acheson, *Morning and Noon* (Boston: Houghton Mifflin, 1965), p. 25.
11. Louis McBurney, *Every Pastor Needs a Pastor* (Waco, TX: Word Books, 1977), p. 151.
12. Steve Mills, "The Image Of Dad, Or The Original Me?," *Baylor Lariat*, Sept. 22, 1981, p. 2.
13. Peter John Marshall, *John Doe, Disciple* (Carmel, NY: Guideposts Associates, 1954), p. 6.
14. Karen Kane, "Several Men Inspired Leon Jaworski," *Houston Chronicle Magazine*, Dec. 5, 1982.
15. Guy Greenfield, *The Wounded Parent* (Grand Rapids, MI: Baker Book House, 1982), p. 26.

In Times of Crisis

Friends were saying goodbye to a little lady at her nursing home. "Have a good week," they said.

"Well, if I can make it till Thursday, I'll make it through the week," she said.

"How do you figure that?" they asked.

Her answer: "I always *have*."

If we could embrace her philosophy, we'd be better able to handle the crisis periods of our lives.

If you live a normal life span, you will encounter many crises; you will grow old, you will know about illnesses and infirmities, you will lose loved ones, you will even go through the less traumatic times of seeing your children leave home, retiring and moving from place to place.

But there are among us—and you may be one of them—those who will suffer grief that is not the expected or routine part of being born, living and dying. Crises can last for years or a lifetime.

Certainly one of these unexpected perils is the preponderance of unhealthy marriages in our society, among clergy as well as laity. If you are there, you know the signs. One wife said she brought the problems on herself; she started out loaded for bear, very distrusting of the church. "So when my husband came home late, I'd say, 'Ah ha, they've taken you away from me again.' If he left the house to minister to someone in need, I accused him of choosing that person over me. After about a year of this, I was a complaining, neurotic wreck, and my husband was completely baffled by the whole affair."

Donna Sinclair tells about a wife whose husband brought on the marital stress—and Donna insists that his strategy is not as uncommon as we might think. This particular husband said to his wife, at the beginning of their marriage, that his responsibility to the church came first, before his wife, before any children they might have. He told her he loved her, but "the family will have to have of me what the church can spare."[1] The poor wife was primed for alienation before it even happened.

Joe McKeever was pastor of an active church in Mississippi when the split *almost* came between him and his wife. For seventeen years their marriage had suffered from "a lack of honest sharing of inner feelings, which also made it impossible to be honest with themselves." Finally Joe informed his church leaders that he planned to file for divorce. That, according to Joe, is when the healing began. The church staff started ministering to him, and members gave emotional support. It was many months before the McKeevers knew their marriage was on solid ground. Looking back, they summarize the convictions that came to them during this time:

1. "You have time to do what you want to do. It's a cop-out for a minister to think he is subject to unrealistic time demands."
2. "Our problems were personal; we could no longer blame someone else; the church was not the culprit."

3. "It's very important for the two of us to be on the same team."
4. "We can decline some invitations and sometimes say the pastor is not available."
5. "Our two hours of scheduled time together each week (usually for lunch somewhere) is so simple, yet so satisfying."
6. "You can depend on God when the bottom drops out."[2]

The pastor's wife has a unique problem when her marriage is in trouble, not just because her husband is a pastor, but because he is *her* pastor. Janet said she has had more than one friend, at such times, say it would be a relief to be able to attend some other church, that it's antagonizing to hear the holy words from a husband when you're angry at him.

William Hulme says it's hard on the husband too. "He feels defeated and insincere....It is difficult for him to preach, knowing she is angry and is listening to what he is saying."[3]

Janet said, "I just plain didn't go to church one Sunday for that very reason. But that's the only time I let things go that far. Usually I can do quite well by using the time to pray or look at the beautiful windows or concentrate on something else. But I'll have to admit I usually get caught up in the sermon and listen even though I don't intend to."

Any of these hurts—being angry on Sunday, accusing each other, not communicating, indulging in snippy arguments (someone has said women nag, men needle)—should not be allowed to fester. Janet says that even though Sunday is supposed to be a high spiritual day, she and Tom have had to use many Sabbath afternoons to settle grievances. "Sometimes things can't wait till Monday."

If your marriage gets stale or you see signs of trouble, initiate some changes. Take a mini vacation, one planned long in advance so you can anticipate it. Get a sitter, if you need one, and go out for the evening. Stay up until your husband gets home in the evening; have breakfast with him in the morning. Have some *good* conversation; don't run off at the mouth. Remember that good timing works wonders. Solomon said that a beautiful woman without good sense is like a gold ring in a pig's snout! Then if, as Janie said, you're "prayed up" and all else fails, get professional help. Don't give up until you've done that.

One minister's wife, whose marriage didn't make it, says the problems are more clear now than they were then. "I felt he was being affirmed each day in his work, getting the physical and the verbal pats on the back. I was driving car pools and going to the grocery store, preparing meals with him in mind, not knowing if he'd be there to eat them. I was sure *I* was the one who needed the ego boost; actually, *he* was the one who needed it."

The national divorce rate is now 50 percent, and the highest rate of increase is among the clergy. Researchers point out that in the past decade, while divorce rates were doubling, the number of women in the work force has increased by 50 percent. Now we can't sit here and say that the working wife is the cause of it all, but, if you are one, it might be good to check out some theories afloat. And if you're not a working wife, the same theories will apply. Those who've made a career of studying the situation tell us that the wife with her own job has "a way out" and many have opted to use it, choosing singleness over marriage. They say our mobile society has taken some of the "disgrace" out of divorce. The "I'm just passing through" theory relieves one of having to face a community of relatives and old-timers with the news of the breakup.

There are those who say divorce is contagious; one couple does it and it goes through a church or a business or a family.

A report presented recently to the Academy of Management pointed out that demands on modern marriages are horrendous, especially among two-career couples. "These demands may include the husband's jealousy or threatened identity; need to share housekeeping and child-raising obligations; up-set in in-laws; feelings of competition between spouses; individual career demands; and simply exhaustion of either or both spouses."[4]

Even though divorce is more common and possibly more acceptable now, it still can ruin a minister's career and often his life. Like it or not, we have a tiger by the tail, according to psychologist Robert Stout, writing in *Christianity Today*. A survey of divorced pastors in the Presbyterian Church U. S. showed that 87 percent felt their divorce had hampered their careers. Richard Morgan of Lenoir, North Carolina, who did the study, wrote in his conclusion, "These ministers felt that they still struggled with the stigma of their broken marriages and remained semi-social outcasts, pariahs to their peers and perceived as misfits."[5]

We're seeing an influx of professional counselors, trained to help ministers and wives avoid marriage breakdowns and to work with them if the efforts fail. Fortunately, children also are considered victims when their parents separate, and counselors take this into consideration. Our son-in-law spent two years working with emotionally disturbed children in a hospital setting; he found that the large majority of these came from broken homes.

"Living alone is not what it's cracked up to be," said a recently divorced minister's wife. "Before, I spent evenings waiting for my husband to come home, heaven knows when; but now I spend my evenings knowing he won't be coming home."

We spoke briefly in chapter 4 about "the other woman," but no discussion on crises in the ministry would be complete without including her. A large-city pastor said you can't be a pastor and refuse to counsel anyone—certainly not because that person happens to be a woman. He also believes that "if things are right at home," counseling women is not dangerous. Most intrigues between ministers and women of the church—and out of the church—come as the result of counseling. You need to understand how this happens. Charles Rassieur wrote an entire book about it. He explains that the woman who loses control is usually lonely and has no one who really cares for her sexually. She goes for counseling and falls in love with the one who may be the first strong male figure in her life: the pastor. The problem is, says Rassieur, that ministers "have a sexual appeal to women, one tied to their roles and professional function...and there are women who manipulate for affection and approval, men to whom the situation is often flattering."[6]

Cathy says she has observed that some women (especially those who feel a bit insecure about themselves) see the minister as a challenge, thus the frequent play for the preacher.

Yet most men, husbands included, are with women day in and out in the business and professional world. I certainly wouldn't want my husband to give up his marvelous secretary or the other women who help him in his work simply because I read into all these relationships a physical involvement. I will admit right here in bold print that my husband is very fond of women and much at ease with them. I couldn't begin to name all the women in his life: patients he visits regularly at the cancer hospital; several widows and divorcees who depend on him for financial counsel and friendship; college students whom he recruits for his company; neighbors, relatives and family. If I spent time worrying about these associations, I certainly wouldn't have time to be sitting here writing about them.

So don't accuse your husband of "leading them on" or "lapping up the attention"; it won't help your home life or your sex life and, besides, the idea might just camp there and make him even more vulnerable for attack.

Yet, when it comes down to fighting for your husband, do it with aplomb, but do it. One minister's wife told me she fought once; she encountered the designing woman with her husband and "what I said to her at that moment would have given the congregation ample reason to dechurch me!"

As we grow older and, as Mrs. Westmoreland said, wiser, we go to the flip side, and life has a familiar new sound. If we have a plan B, now is the time to use it. As the proverb goes, "It's no use to wait for your ship to come in, unless you have sent one out." I can remember when I was young and saved all my gifts—linens, perfumes, dishes—but no more; I can hardly wait to put them to use. And yet we never grow up completely; there's always a bit of the child in us—to keep the fun and the love of life in our mature years. No person is entirely free of childish characteristics, "not even the most distinguished psychoanalysts," according to the noted psychiatrist Dr. Paul Tournier. So growing old can't be all bad.

We know, of course, there are perils in growing old, that our bodies slow down, infirmities come. (An elderly friend told me recently she just hopes her teeth last as long as she does, that some people worry about their eyes or their ears, but good teeth are not to be taken lightly.) Those of us still busy and productive can only imagine about the years ahead of us, but we can attempt to be prepared. The Psalmist says we can still "yield fruit in old age."

Letters from my 81-year-old mother are chronicles of her weekly activities: two parties this week, one shower, a tea, the symphony, a funeral or two, the study club, the 84 club, the Week of Prayer, the BALL (Be Active, Live Longer) Club and, of course, church four times a week. A friend asked her recently what was the best time of her life and she said, "Right now." On her 75th birthday, my brother George called and greeted her with, "Well, Mother, how does it feel to be 75?" She answered, "Considering the alternative, it feels great." All this in spite of the fact that her life has been fraught with many burdens, including widowhood at age 49 and the death two years ago of a much loved son. She is a "right now" woman.

Grief comes in many forms, but most of us, when we hear the word "grief," think immediately of the death of a loved one.

A friend wrote to us of the death of her younger sister: "She chose to come home to die. All four of her sisters have been with her for the last two weeks of her life. When she died, her husband was holding her, and her three sons were all on the bed with her. It was a beautiful picture of family love."

But we must grieve. As Jacob said, "If I am bereaved, then I am bereaved." We are told that we should not be surprised or disappointed with ourselves when we grieve; it is our right, it is expected, it is necessary.

Early in my preparation for this book, Minette Drumwright shared with me many insights about the life of a minister's wife. She talked about her childhood as the daughter of a pastor, of her life with her minister husband and the high points and low points of their life together. She spoke of their daughters and how they were "a source of ecstatic joy" to their parents, of the new home and new field of service in Arkansas. Life was good, and I could feel that as she talked.

A year later, her husband died. Less than two weeks after his death, Minette spoke to a group of church leaders at a Service of Reflection honoring his memory. From the text of that speech I have chosen this portion:

"I am frustrated by my loss—by our loss—oh, I know it's temporary—but it's reality. I am confused, I don't understand. He had so much to do and to be and to give.

"But please hear this. In the midst of loss and grief, I can say with every fiber of my hurting being that underneath *are* the everlasting arms, that the Lord is my God and I *am* trusting him.

"I am awed by the peace I have felt. Huber and I lived it together—a lifestyle of peace. It was as natural as breath itself. But this crisis and trauma and heartbreak have introduced me to a whole new dimension of that peace that passes understanding. It works, my friends, it works. He is able."

There is one thing I must tell you about grief that I have learned from my research. Many marriages do not hold together after the death of a child; some statistics go as high as 50 percent. This is an enigma to me; it seems to me that this is the time when we need to comfort each other, to help each other survive the future. Milton Ferguson, whose sixteen-year-old daughter was killed in an automobile accident, understands this phenomenon, even though he and his wife have been great support to each other. He explains that couples often do not, possibly *cannot*, verbalize their grief to each other at such times, and this deprivation eats away at the marriage relationship.

When Harry, a friend of our family, was killed, I called my brother Mike to give him the message. He said, "Death is so much a part of life, isn't it?" And so it is. But you too have the Everlasting Arms.

My husband and I are continually in touch with people in crisis situations because of poor health: families who have come to the medical center in Houston for cancer treatment. These people leave their homes, leave children in the care of friends and relatives, borrow money, take leaves of absence from jobs and often lose jobs, travel by car and plane back and forth from cities hundreds of miles away. They often sleep and exist in small hospital rooms. All this in order to be with a loved one who is a patient in the hospital. Poor health can take its toll not only on the patient but also on the family. This is crisis! It's critical also when the patient is at home or when the patient happens to be you.

Obviously, some illnesses are more serious than others, some are even emotionally induced, and how we handle them is pretty much predetermined by our fortitude and the kind of support we get from our family and friends. A friend was diagnosed as having a possibly terminal illness. Her physical survival was due to many factors, but, she said, "My emotional survival is due, pure and simple, to the support of my family and the people of the church."

Jean Ford, whose mouth and throat were paralyzed by polio when she was a child, started making public speeches only recently. Up until then she was not confident about her speech; she had had to have a great deal of therapy to regain her voice and learn how to swallow. Even now her voice is weak and she has a small speech impediment. But she says that just as God told Moses He would be his mouth, "so He is being mine."[7]

I read of a manic-depressive who survived by "really" reading her Bible in the psychiatric hospital and learning to release her fears and worries to the Lord.

You've heard of the remarkable recovery to health of Norman Cousins, who declares he cured his terminal illness largely through laughter. In his best-seller, *Anatomy of an Illness*, he reports that ten minutes of good, hearty laughter would give him two hours of sleep without pain. Continuing this process, he eventually was free of his disease.

The Chinese people are fond of the saying, "If I hang a green bough in my heart, the singing bird will surely come."

A friend talked with me about what it's like to have an imperfect child, what you do with your grief, how you carry on. She says prayer helps, it really does, but it's not enough.

"Then what would you say to the mother of an imperfect child?" I asked.

And her answer was twofold: "First, talk about it. You absolutely must talk about it. Then, never blame each other. We never have," she said, "to this day—and it's been twenty-five years."

Recently I attended a very large state meeting at which Ruth Landes Pitts was the soloist, and I remembered again the first time I saw her, how I sat amazed as she performed the piano accompaniment for our church choir. You would have to see this remarkable woman to understand my amazement.

Ruth was born with only four fingers and only one leg. A series of operations created a third finger on her right hand and straightened her left leg for a brace. Prosthesis gave her a right leg. With all this accomplished, Ruth had, for all practical purposes, two usable fingers on each hand. The miracle of it is that she became an accomplished pianist, a performing vocalist, a college teacher, a wife and mother.

Speaking of her parents, Ruth said, "Although I'm sure they must have had a tremendous adjustment to make following my birth, they have had a beautifully Christian attitude toward my defects, and since I grew up with the problem, it never seemed a handicap."[8]

All the soldiers were like each other except one, who was a little different; he had only one leg, for he was the last to be cast, and there was not enough tin, but he stood just as steadily on his one leg as the others on their two. And it was just this one little soldier that became famous.

—"The Brave Tin Soldier," *Andersen's Fairy Tales*

"Clergy burnout" is a rather new phrase in our culture, but it represents a real form of distress. Janie understands it; she said, "Bob went through a stagnant period. Talk about grief!" Carol Wilson said Charles, early in his ministry, had a case of clergy burnout, but it wasn't because he was stagnant; it was more that he didn't have time to do the ministering because of being bogged down in administration. "Every day he'd come home and say, 'Well, I didn't have time to study today either; I was caught up in office work, as usual.' It wasn't until we moved from that church that he regained his enthusiasm."

A recent study indicates that a big reason for clergy burnout is the gap between a congregation's needs and the clergyman's skills, especially in the area of counseling. Still another survey says it's because the pastor and the congregation so often have different ideas about priorities: evangelism versus stewardship, youth ministries versus adult ministries, music versus administration, etc. In the end, it all comes down to a personal problem, each minister with his own feelings, his own identity. Maybe it's because of anxiety over lack of accomplishments, competition with other ministers, a sense of inferiority, doubt about his calling, poor devotional and study time, unsatisfactory prayer life.

The trouble with clergy burnout is that so often it leads to abandoning the ministry. Most ministers who leave their profession are in the 30-40 age bracket and pastor churches of less than 300 members, which says to us that there are *some* in larger churches and some in different age brackets who are making the break.

And all these exits can't be blamed on clergy burnout. Quite often it's because the minister just can't balance his church job and family problems. Janie says she has known wives who actually became ill because they couldn't handle the stresses of their role, and many times the husband would decide to chuck it all and get some other kind of job.

"I had a friend at the seminary," said Gina, "who was a really neat person, lots going for her and all. But the one thing that always bothered me about her was that she really didn't want to be a preacher's wife. Once she said to me, 'I don't think I'd mind so much if he were a music director or a counselor or something, but I hate telling people I'm a *preacher*'s wife.' Sure enough, about five years later, we heard that he had left the ministry and was going back to school."

My lawyer brother, Don, recently had clients who were involved in a divorce settlement; their problem was that *she* didn't want to be married to a preacher and *he* refused to quit preaching.

What can you, the wife and helpmeet, do when you sense the onset of clergy burnout? You can do what Janie did—pray a lot. You can be sure you're an available sounding board. You can give him the freedom to make some decisions without being over-whelmed by what *you* think he should or should not do; your ideas may conflict with countless others he is having to listen to.

Church members were having their pastor and his wife in their home for dinner one evening. When all their guests arrived, some-one suggested that the pastor might like to take off his tie. "No, thank you," he responded, "that's all that's holding my head on."

Sometimes the pastor doesn't have even a tie. And maybe, again, this is where you come in, helping him keep his head on his shoulders. Tell him you've read (because you're about to read it) that sometimes ministers need help from fellow pastors or from professional counselors. Wise men suggest that young ministers should try to find older ministers for supportive therapy.

Most cities have organizations for the gathering of ministers (within denominations and in combination with various denominations) to discuss church problems. We are seeing healthy signs that these same groups are enlarging their agendas to include dialogues on *personal* problems. There is a rapidly expanding network of Christian counseling centers; there are centers and counselors specializing in the problems of ministers. Books are available in all bookstores to help the man who is suffering emotionally and otherwise. Try to find a ministering group that includes couples and go with your husband; in helping him, you'll help yourself.

"But don't go outside the Christian community for help," said Ruth. "I've seen some people get really messed up that way. Don't substitute the occult and humanism and things like that for Christianity."

Finally, as Kenneth Chafin put it, "Trying to make it without God is like playing basketball in your bathrobe."

Studies about the needs of ministers and their churches reveal confusion in Christian attitudes toward conflict. For example, is conflict inevitable in close relationships? Is conflict wrong? What should be the Christian's reaction to conflict? The North Carolina group said their study showed a great need for theological as well as practical assistance.

Carlyle Marney answered some of these questions when he said, "There can be no moral life without tension. The words of tension— choice, distinction, freedom in evil, free will—all mean that moral life is shot through with tension....All moral life is a part of the tragedy and drama of choice."[9]

The tragedy and drama of choice. Jim had been at his church about five years when he was "put on notice" by a group of deacons. His children didn't understand the evening's church proceedings exactly and they were hurt, but they "were not threatened." The family weathered that storm. When the night came for the vote on censuring the pastor, Jim was given a vote of confidence by more than two-thirds of the membership.

I asked what they had done during those days between the announcement and the vote. "Nothing," said his wife, "except pray as usual; we just stayed out of the Lord's way and let Him take care of it."

Stacy Harrison's family didn't fare as well when their church took a vote. Stacy's father was "voted out." "We just didn't get enough votes to stay," her father said. The church gave them three months to get out of the parsonage; the mother had to take a tiring, poor-paying job; the supportive grandfather came down with cancer, which devastated the four children; and when, after three months, the father still had not found a church, the family moved into a mobile home, six of them in two bedrooms. Eventually Donald Harrison did get a new church assignment, but even before then, Stacy had written about their experiences.

"The past year, my senior year, has been one of the greatest years of my life. I have learned something that isn't taught in textbooks. I have seen faith work. My attitude has become new. I know that I will face many more problems ahead, but now I have some real experiences to look back on and remember."[10]

We all have fears. Being Christian does not keep us from being afraid. And these times of consternation can serve a purpose in our lives. Often our fears keep us from getting into trouble, like the child who avoids the oncoming care because he realizes he may be hurt if he doesn't get out of the way.

"I was so frightened the first time I sang a solo in our little church," said Denise, "that I practiced for days! But it paid off and I was as cool as a cucumber and sang quite well really."

So use your fears. He who burns his mouth blows his soup.

"But what do you do when you make a mess of things—" asked Gina, "when you really foul up? You can't go back and do it over again. I think you need to speak to this; many wives suffer from one goof-up after another."

Well, we all have feet of clay. The bungling wives need to remember this. To err is human. If they could just look inside other people's lives, they'd see they're not so different. We all put our best faces forward as much as possible and hide our misdemeanors, so we see ours but we don't see the other person's. Also, each wife needs to look inside her own self and ask, "Why am I all thumbs? Why do I always put my feet in my mouth?"—or whatever—and then get busy with some changes. Like allowing more time, using shortcuts, limiting phone calls, cleaning house, thinking before speaking. With a little self-probing we come up with ways to improve ourselves. Then, of course, it's okay to cry a lot and pray a lot; that helps too.

I met Becky at a bookstore opening and, in the course of our conversation, I asked her what she had found to be her biggest problem as a minister's wife. She was still a very young wife, but her answer showed wisdom beyond her years. "Loneliness," she said. "Definitely my biggest problem. And it was because of my destructive thought patterns that I was lonely. I would sit at home alone and keep thinking to myself 'here I am alone and my husband is gone' over and over and over. And during that time I did the very worst thing; I read romantic novels! Can you believe? Here I sit, a newlywed, more or less, pining away for my husband and I read romantic novels!"

Becky got up and got out of her trap largely by taking advice from her mother to "get out and do things for people." And the reason I was seeing her on a Saturday morning in a bookstore was that she had shared with her husband not only the pain of her loneliness but also her intention to change her course—and part of their rescue plan was to spend their Saturdays doing what *she* wanted to do.

Wives in small churches and in small towns are plagued with loneliness more than are those in our cities. A common cry goes out: "The people in this town don't need new friends; they don't want me." That's when *you* have to make the moves. Invite them into your home. Oh yes, you can. If a holiday is approaching, use that as justification for a coffee klatsch or a cookie exchange. Watch for reasons to write notes to people: new babies (to grandparents as well as to parents), anniversaries, illnesses, a thank-you for anything. I remember the two young teen-agers in our church who were so enraptured with our new recreation director that they made a batch of cookies and took it to him at his home; then when he wrote them a thank-you note, they wrote him a thank-you note thanking him for the thank-you note! Ask people for their recipes, their ideas, their solutions. Ellen Jones says it's much more effective to ask someone to decorate your house for you than it is to say, "My, you're so creative."

Recently I was listening on my car radio to a station that plays songs familiar to me when I was much younger, and I heard the song "Alone Again, Naturally," the words of which I knew quite well once (now I know I just mouthed them; I certainly didn't contemplate them). The last verse says,

> God, in his mercy,
>   Left me in my time of need;
> Now I'm alone
>   Naturally.[11]

I'm here to tell you it isn't so; He won't leave you in your time of need, and you won't be alone.

There seem always to be times when you are feeling low and someone tells you to snap out of it, to pull yourself together, and you don't know how to snap and you don't know how to pull. And sometimes you're not even sure that this is the time to snap and pull. Martha Nelson says she asked a specialist this once, how you know when you need help, what are the warning signs. And the answer came back,

> When she is depressed and wants to stay in, away from things; when she is very angry without being able to put her fingers on why; when the feeling grows that she really does not want to go to church; when she begins to pick up on every little thing people say to her; when she is sick a lot with backaches, stomachaches, headaches; and when she cries a

lot—these are signs she may need some medical help with the strain she is under.[12]

Some of these may apply to you, and some may not. See a doctor about your physical problems; he should be able to give you sources of help for the others.

Without exception, every time I asked a minister's wife for advice to pass on to you about getting out of the doldrums or handling the really big disorders, she said to tell you to set aside a time to pray. Now that's different from just praying, and it's different from the family devotion at the dinner table, even though that may be a set time. What they want to tell you is: this should be your place and your time—alone. Anne Ortlund said that when she was encompassed by diapers, bottles and desperation, she promised the Lord that if he'd help her, she'd get up at 3:00 o'clock every morning and spend some time with him. "I kept my tryst with him until the schedule lightened; I didn't die; and I'm not sorry I did it."[13]

Now that her time is more her own, Anne, with her husband, takes off an entire day each month—goes out of town usually—and spends the time praying, evaluating and planning.

"Oh, I've wanted to do that," said Janet. "Many times I've said to Tom I think it would be great to go away for a whole day somewhere where it's quiet and peaceful—and pray. Tom suggested that I just stay up all *night* here at home and pray, that it would be peaceful and quiet. Even though it was one of his crafty suggestions, I've become intrigued with the idea and some night soon I'm going to do it!"

It's right to get excited about prayer. It will guide you in youth, support you in maturity, comfort you in old age.

Several years ago I visited an eighty-year-old friend in the hospital, where she was recuperating from surgery. She gave a treatise on prayer that morning that I remember often. She said, "When you can't see very well and you can't hear very well and you can't read and you can't listen, it surely is good to be able to pray and quote scriptures."

When Ruth Graham lost consciousness after falling out of a tree, she found that she could not remember a single Bible verse. "Suddenly," she said, "I felt as a man must feel who learns the bank has failed and he has lost his life savings. 'Lord,' I begged, 'You can have anything I've got, but please give me back my Bible verses.'"[14]

In the hospital room, at the kitchen sink, on the busy freeway, prayer is always there for our remembering; God is always there for the hearing.

My brother Durward was visiting our older brother Harry and the two of them were preparing to spend ten minutes in the sauna where Harry went each day. Durward asked him how, without a watch, he'd know when it had been ten minutes. "That's how long it takes me," said Harry, "to repeat the 23rd Psalm, the 13th chapter of First Corinthians and to pray the Lord's Prayer."

Make prayer a habit, a tool, a source of help, a shout of gladness. Find your place and your time; be alone.

> Tears may linger at nightfall,
> but joy comes in the morning.
>
> —Psalm 30:5, NEB

NOTES

1. Donna Sinclair, *The Pastor's Wife Today* (Nashville: Abingdon, 1981), p. 23.
2. Chronicle News Service, "Reconciliation in the Parsonage," *Houston Chronicle*, May 9, 1981.

3. William Hulme, *Your Pastor's Problems* (Minneapolis: Augsburg, 1977), p. 77.

4. Joe A. Cox and Kris Moore, *Divorce and the Dual Career: Perceptions of Career Women* (Waco, TX: Baylor University Press, 1981), p. 1.

5. George W. Cornell, "Divorce Among Clergy More Common, But Still A Stigma," *Houston Post*, March 27, 1982.

6. Charles Rassieur, *The Problem Clergymen Don't Talk About* (Philadelphia: Westminster, 1976), p. 61.

7. Dr. A. J. Armstrong, "Mistletoe and Holly for Christmas," *Sigma Tau Delta Magazine*, 1947.

8. Pat Dishman, *Ten Who Overcame* (Nashville: Broadman, 1966), p. 91.

9. Carlyle Marney, *Priests to Each Other* (Valley Forge, PA: Judson Press, 1978), p. 88.

10. Stacey Harrison, "Our Time of Testing," *Guideposts*, July 1982, p. 33.

11. Raymond O'Sullivan, "Alone Again, Naturally" (M.A.M. Publishing, 1972).

12. Martha Nelson, *This Call We Share* (Nashville: Broadman, 1977).

13. Anne Ortlund, *Disciplines of the Beautiful Woman* (Waco, TX: Word Books, 1980), p. 29.

14. Ruth Bell Graham, *It's My Turn* (Minneapolis: Grason, 1982), p. 171.

8

Your Own Best Self

It was the first day of kindergarten for Lynn Elaine, whose family called her Elaine. When she returned home that day, she told her mother that the teacher kept calling her Lynn. She mentioned this several times until, finally, the mother asked, "Well, does that bother you so much, Elaine? Do you really object to the teacher's calling you Lynn?"

"No," answered Elaine, "but I wish she'd call me Marietta."

When my friend told me this story, we agreed that there are times when, if there were a choice, we'd all like to be someone else. There are Mariettas in our lives who appear to be improvements over us. Yet we must live with and within ourselves.

I pray for you as I write this chapter. Since we all have problems, I know you do also. You're lonely or tired or discouraged; you're battling jealousy, maybe guilt; you don't like the way you look or move or sound; you have all the aches and pains in the book. And no one cares. It's a gloomy picture, but it can change. It has—for many ministers' wives. The beautiful you is there: God sees it; you and the rest of us want to see it too.

Musician Lester Lanin said his dad always told him, "Son, there isn't a person in the world with your fingerprints. So be yourself and set your own style."[1] If your father didn't say that to you, he could have. You are unique; no one is just like you.

And yet we are all enough alike that we understand each other and we can help each other. More than one minister's wife suggested to me that I jerk you up by saying to you, "So you're a preacher's wife, so what? Other people are doctors' wives and lawyers' wives and teachers' wives." Janet said, "Look, I know it's rough sometimes, really rough. But I think we become stagnant too; we live in the world of ministers' wives until all we see are copies of ourselves. We need to move out and meet wives in the other world." Ruth advocates not referring to yourself as a minister's wife or thinking of yourself as one. If asked, respond with "My husband is a pastor," or "My husband directs church music." I do not recall ever saying "I am an accountant's wife." One pastor's wife says that when you come out with that minister's-wife handle, you come across as expecting to be patronized. You are your own person; don't lean on your husband's title.

There is a maxim rampant these days that says "you have to do what you have to do," and though it is often misused, it still holds a truth worth embracing. If you need to make a change in your life, *you* have to do it. For a time, a beautiful, talented friend fought and suffered with a poor self-image. I remember once when she was going through a very difficult time, falling backwards most times when she tried to go forward, that her husband said, "The hardest part is that I can't do it *for* her; she has to do it herself."

In her book *Disciplines of the Beautiful Woman*, Anne Ortlund says that after she had been a pastor's wife for twenty years, she began to get "thirstier and thirstier" for more of God in her life. Therein lies the secret. Let God in on it. And you may have to let other people in on it too. Denise Fry said that over and over again she tried to lose weight by keeping her diets secret. Finally she realized that she could stay with her program only when she had some confidantes, when she let it be known that she was attempting to lose weight. "People will really help you if they know you're trying. They won't force the goodies on you, they'll understand when you turn down certain foods, and they'll support you by applauding your progress."

Most ministers' wives do eventually have to fight the battle of the bulge. And I found that a lot of them place the blame on the church itself. "We just can't do anything at our church," said Denise, "without eating. We have donuts with coffee, we have trays of cookies at committee meetings, we have 'refreshments' at the drop of a hat." The minister's wife—and all other smart wives—must learn to pass these by.

Denise said the real turnabout with her obesity came with the realization that she was a "hypocrite, plain as day. I was giving a lot of devotions in Sunday School departments and my prevailing theme was 'God can change me, he can change you' and there I stood, forty pounds overweight. My listeners certainly had reason to ask, 'Then, why doesn't he change your size?' On the morning that all of this hit me, I had used a scripture from Second Samuel that said, 'I will not give God that which costs me nothing!' I knew it would cost me to lose weight, but I did it. I gave God and myself the gift of a healthy body, and now when I stand before a group, they can believe in the miracles of God!"

I read from one expert recently who said you can eat everything you want *if* you exercise enough! When you calculate that it takes two miles of brisk walking to burn up the calories from one piece of chocolate cake, you're faced with the choice of less cake or more walking. Yet proper nutrition and exercise are far more than just losing weight; they are essentials of good health. By taking care of these Holy Ghost temples we are more able to resist and fight off infections, recuperate from illnesses and garner the strength we need for our daily rounds.

One physical fitness professional wrote, "The key elements of wellness are knowing the purpose of life, understanding its genuine joys and pleasures and assuming total and complete self-responsibility."

Zerrissenheit is a German word for "torn-to-pieces-hood." Even though you probably never have come right out and said it, you're bound to feel *Zerrissenheit* once in a while. There are times when everything seems to come down on you at once.

Gina Ross went through one really big, bad scene—lots of little ones, you understand, but this was a *big* one. "Frank was the director of youth and music and some of his teen-agers had started coming by our place at nights, staying late and expecting to be fed. It was the only time Frank and I *could* have had together. By the time the place cleared at nights, we were exhausted and went to bed without having the talking time we really needed. I was angry at Frank and he was angry at me for being angry. During this time one of the ladies of the church complained to me about the kind of music the young people were singing and another made a caustic remark about my influence on my husband's theology. It was a Wednesday night and I flew home in a rage and paced the floor until Frank came in. Then I let him have it with both barrels! It was an eruption he couldn't ignore and go to bed on.

"Looking back on it, we chalk the whole thing up to what Frank calls being 'amateurs of the trade.' If we had been more experienced, we would have seen to it that the teen-agers gathered at the church or at their own homes, and if I had not been so uptight, I could have sloughed off the innuendoes of the people at the church. And, of course, if Frank and I had been more attuned to the problems each of us was going through, the whole thing could have been avoided."

Gina feels that she is not plagued with guilt such as she sees in many of her counterparts; if she were, the situation—and all situations—would have been compounded. I was listening to a radio talk show when a woman called in to speak with the guest psychologist. She said she had been raised in a home lorded over by a hard-line preacher-father, "but," she confessed, "I thought, at age sixty-two, I had buried all the guilt feelings of blaming my father and using him as the excuse for my lack of self-esteem. But the depression keeps returning and I'm beginning to feel it will be with me till I die." This woman should have talked with a professional years before. Her turned-inward anger should have been turned out and dealt with.

Most studies dealing with guilt give two major suggestions: (1) stop doing whatever it is that you feel guilty about and replace it with something you feel good about, and (2) remember that guilt feelings are not so much guilt as they are disappointment and/or anger.

Then there's loneliness. Janet says everything gets exaggerated when you're lonely, so you absolutely must avoid loneliness. Which is easier said than done, according to Janet. "Some people sit at home alone because their pride won't let them 'impose' themselves on other people. Some wives are frightened to be alone, and some don't know how to improvise, to read or get involved in a project. Some are not aware of the value of friendships."

Ruth Senter says she is afraid ministers' wives are creating "lofty, lonely positions" for themselves by eliminating the need for others. She says, "One thing that smashed my pastor's wife fantasy was that business hours for the pastor are often night hours. When the honeymoon ended, I found myself with many empty evenings and I began to feel ignored and neglected....I decided to change my agenda for evenings."[2]

It is really difficult to believe that in modern times and in modern churches, the average minister's wife cannot find resources for adding to the enjoyment of life. A friend who lives in a small town told me that her pastor's wife, in an effort to combat the smallness and possible boredom of the town, drives sixty miles into the city twice a month. "I happen to know," said the friend, "that she usually goes to a movie, eats lunch in a good restaurant and shops or visits the museums. I think it's great and I can't imagine that anyone would object to it."

I heard of another wife who marks off the 15th of each month on her calendar; that is *her* day to do *her* thing, whatever way-out or lazy thing that might be.

Much of the advice to ministers' wives these days seems to lean heavily on the admonition that it is more important to learn to say no to the people of the church than it is to say yes. Unfortunately, this borders on negative thinking and a negative way of responding to people who generally love you and whom you are learning to love. But there is merit in knowing when you're doing enough and even too much and using graceful means to preserve a rational lifestyle. It's a lesson we all have to learn, and we don't want to unbalance the scale in the direction of underdoing any more than we want to weight it toward overdoing. The secret has to be in how we feel about what we're doing. No doubt, the small town pastor's wife's anticipation of her two days a month in the city made the other days more satisfying.

Boredom and all the cynical and downbeat emotions it triggers will color your myriad relationships. Your marriage will suffer, your children will mimic your disposition, and big and little things will become distorted.

Carol Wilson saw it happening in her life. "I guess it showed up most in the bedroom," she said. "Our sex life was the pits, really. Charles was tired, I was tired. I was not my usual jovial self; everything was so downright serious. I knew my responsibilities as a Christian wife, the submitting part and all that, but most of the time I wished I didn't know it. I had to get help to get out of that one!"

Dr. Bertha Bunda, director of social services at Hinds General Hospital in Jackson, Mississippi, is quoted as saying, "I'm convinced about these courses in submission: every time I see a sweet young thing trying to follow the instructions, I know that somewhere out there things are going to collapse; there's going to be an explosion. She is simply burying feelings that must be worked through."[3]

Carol clarified that her "help" was not a course in submission, but, as Dr. Bunda said, it had to be worked through. "My self-image was drooping at that point, and when I learned to like myself, everything else eventually fell into place."

One young wife was having a hard time because she didn't like to stay alone at night. She was especially afraid of storms when she was alone. If she or someone in her family became ill, she panicked. She had nightmares about her husband's leaving her. She still battles with some of these problems, but she is making progress. "I am *never* alone anymore," she said. "I have two pre-schoolers and they certainly keep me company at nights when my husband is gone. Sometimes I even wish for time alone and that confirms an emotional victory, and I get really excited." She has prayed a great deal about her insecurity and gives God the credit for her improvement. And as one long-term minister's wife said, "There is only one way to learn to pray and that is to pray."

Even though we put prayer at the top of our list of helps, there are other supports, most of them actually a part of or the result of prayer. There is a time to weep and a time to laugh and, as someone said, heaven help the minister's wife who cannot do both.

Frances Bradsher was telling about an incident in her childhood when her sister had a broken finger. "As soon as it happened, Papa took her on his lap, waiting for Mother to call the doctor. He pressed her head against his shoulder expecting her to cry, I suppose. She looked awkward sitting there, straight and white, like she hadn't sat on anybody's lap before. She looked at me hard, as a sympathetic tear rolled down my cheek. Grandmother always said no lady cries in public, but Harriet was trembling now and I wished I knew how to tell her the way tears washed the trembling away."[4]

Probably you have heard that you really haven't lived your life to its fullest if you have not experienced the emotions that designate you as a human being. You need to stretch those feelings, much as one fills and stretches a balloon, to sense the potential of them. To feel the exhilaration of being praised, to know the agony of rejection—both are your lot. It is important to learn that crying "washes the trembling away" and that riotous laughter is good for the soul. You need to experience the frustration of anger, the depths of losing and winning, the pain of death, the joy of birth. To be carried to the heights of heaven by beautiful music will stir your heart as it was designed to be stirred, as will the tugging of great sermons, orations, drama and contests. That falling-in-love sensation of your youth needs to come into play throughout life for the sheer happiness it brings, but also as a reminder that your emotional responses are intact.

I read about an ancient people who celebrated the rising of the sun, who actually had an annual festival to bless the fact that this miracle happened in their lives. So I decided that I too would celebrate the rising of the sun. I rose before daybreak and took my place in the grandstand of my yard. And there I watched as the ball of fire appeared and, with great drama, ascended in perfect timing and brightening. I could relate to the ancient tribe; there should have been Hallelujah music and a great jubilant shout!

Be receptive to your emotions, celebrate life! Enjoy! Give thanks!

After you pray and cry, yes, and laugh, you still need to talk with *people*. A frightened little boy at bedtime was told by his father, "God loves you and will take care of you." But the little boy answered, "I know, but I want somebody who has skin on."[5]

Janie kept reminding me to tell you just that, that ministers' wives need "pastoral care" just as other wives do, and "if you can't have counseling sessions with your husband, as his members can, then get them somewhere else."

Of course, there are times when the tongue needs to be bridled, when too many people in too many places have heard too many churchyard elegies. As Carol said of one of her friends, "If being open helps, she should be emotionally perfect. She has paraded her problem to the entire city and beyond."

A friend described her pastor's wife to me as a person who uses familiar patterns as a way of surviving. She said that you have the feeling she does things in certain ways because she "has always done it that way, knows how to do it that way, and is afraid to try something new or even 'go along.'"

Bruce Larson presents the novel concept that our lives do not contain enough adventure. "You need to choose life in the area of risk and danger. You need to reverse one of the most deadly forces in your life—your inordinate need for safety. Ultimately, that safety is a prison. Let God help you to risk creatively."[6] (Or, as the saying goes, you have to break an egg to make an omelet.)

Gail Sheehy explains what she calls the "euphoria among the *happiest* women." Those with a strong sense of well-being, according to her research, have suffered just as many hardships and losses as have the miserable women. "The critical difference is this: they usually have confronted a difficulty, rocked the boat, picked themselves up, and taken the painful steps necessary to free themselves from what they finally perceived as a trap, self-made or imposed."[7]

Our daughter Dana was excited about facts she had learned in graduate school that said, though in more intellectual terms, that elderly people are what they are because, unrestrained, they have become their "natural" selves. I said, "Oh, Dana, that isn't new. I learned that twenty years ago and did a series of adult devotions on it." I could hardly wait to find my ancient notes and show them to her. There they were, the first one dated "February 7th, 1965, El Ada class." The gist of the whole thing was in paragraph 3, page 2: "The psychiatrist says that older people who display intense, often new, personality traits, are being 'themselves' (in contrast to saying 'they're not themselves'). When a person is young, he can control his emotions, his personality and his actions so as to appear a well-adjusted, congenial, normal person. But as he grows older, his controls are loosened and relaxed—and he becomes what he can't help being. Which is, in reality, what he has been all his life."

So if the fear of growing old is haunting you, now is the time to make emotional provisions. Youth may be a gift of nature, but a beautiful old age is a work of art. Abraham Lincoln said, "Everyone over forty is responsible for his face"—the anger that shows, the turmoil, the boredom.

Helen Hayes, who has grown old wonderfully as well as gracefully, passes on her advice for aging as she has: "I know too many young women today who are desperately searching for themselves, and who have tossed a lot aside to do so. I suppose this business of being in search of yourself is all right, but not to the exclusion of other things, of your duty or your obligations to other people—like spouses and children. I think you can be a free spirit and still be a giving one, and marriage is one long giving on both sides. I don't think there's enough of that today."[8]

One of the ways to get to know yourself—and to like yourself—is to recognize your own gifts, what you have in the way of talents and attributes that are worthy of giving away. Then, just as you would give any other gift, share with others. Do not give in order to receive, but give in order to glow in the joy of others and to become the cheerful, no-holds-barred giver.

It may be that all you need to enhance your self-ego is to look better. If, when you look in the mirror, you see something you don't like, change it. If you can't change it, accept it. The saying is true that "God didn't make any junk," so shine up his masterpiece.

Mr. Leonard is the hairdresser in the book *A Hat on the Hall Table*. A conversation between him and the local pastor's wife goes something like this:

"I'm surprised that you want a new hairdo."

"Why?"

"Well, when you walk up the aisle with this sophisticated new coiffure, aren't you afraid of what people will say?"

"I'm doing this for myself, not for the people of Saint Michael's."

"How is it that you want a change?"

"You just finished telling me that we must keep up with the times, and that's what I'm doing. There's another reason though. My son will say, 'Mommy, you're beautiful,' and my husband will look up and exclaim, 'Honey! You look wonderful!' "[9]

Janet says the few comments she hears about her clothes are just in passing, like "that's a lovely color" or "I love your dress"—never "Where did you find that suit?" or "I can tell you've been shopping," etc. "I was prepared for such comments and questions, though, and I had practiced how I'd say something clever like 'Yes, my annual buying spree' or 'Oh, I've had this a while.' A friend said that no matter what the comment is, she always says simply 'thank you,' which really is the best response."

The wife of a well-known football coach told a gathering of women, "One thing I invest in each year is a new robe. When my husband leaves at 7:00 in the morning, I want him to have good thoughts about me all day."

Fashion designers and retailers give intriguing tips about how, with the use of a new belt or scarf or piece of jewelry, you can dress up last year's—or last decade's—dress, or how an old dress top can be used as a blouse for a new suit, and how with a minimum of separates, you can build a fashionable new wardrobe.

How you dress and walk and wear your hair are just the beginnings of the social graces. They all fall flat if your pleasing personality doesn't come through. There is an announcer on one of our local radio stations who exudes great excitement in giving the mundane announcements of the day. He makes the fact that "it's 8:36" or "twenty minutes before 3:00" sound like Big Ben's first chime since last year.

Conversation is a fine art and you need to develop it. Part of that art is listening, looking people in the eye as they speak, responding accordingly—and not interrupting. A little poem I found, I know not where, says:

> Her thoughts are slow, her words are few
> and never formed to glisten,
> but she is joy to all her friends—
> you should hear her listen.

And always, always, your *manners* are showing. If and how you say "thank you" and "please." The way you eat. Making others feel at ease. Waiting your turn. These sound juvenile and insignificant, but they count for a great deal in the overall picture of your charm, and they are a visible way of working on self-esteem.

And just because you're a minister's wife doesn't mean you have to put restraints on having fun. "The minister's wife can set the tone for amusement," said Ruth Porter. "When I understood this, I made a special effort to loosen up and laugh more. And all around me I could see how it was the cue to unwind that people needed."

I was impressed by a prayer I heard a minister's wife pray many years ago, so impressed that I found it among my notes and clippings recently: "Lord, give us a sense of humor and the grace to see a joke when it presents itself."

Gina "confessed" that she likes to play games: cards, Scrabble, Monopoly, any kind of table game. "But you can imagine that as a pastor's wife, about the only time I can indulge is with my children on cold winter's evenings around the kitchen table. When my sister was visiting me once, we talked about this, and she, knowing my competitive urge, suggested that I arrange to visit her for a few days two or three times a year and she would promise to have people in for long days and evenings of games. And that's exactly what I do. I love it!"

Since I'm the member of the family who doesn't go to school or work 8:00 to 5:00, I'm usually the one delegated to stand in line for tickets to ball games, the circus, the theater, the symphony, whatever. Often if the line is long and the weather is awful, I am tempted to chuck it all and tell my sponsors that it just wasn't worth it. But then comes the evening or the day of the big event and I am glad I stayed in line; it was worth it, after all.

Our daughter-in-law Kathy suffered from a delayed diagnosis of dyslexia. Writing thank-you notes for wedding gifts was a double chore; she'd write, Jon would correct, she or he would rewrite. Then she took a college English course that turned her on. She gained confidence in her abilities, made an A, and now, according to Jon, "she sits over there and reads and reads!"

It takes effort to make the good times happen, but they really are balm for the spirit, as both Jon and Kathy will affirm.

In response to the survey question "Do you feel that a minister's wife's closest friend or friends should be members of her husband's congregation?" one wife wrote, "Impossible. I find that, in our small congregation, this puts undue pressure on the members and on our 'holy' role."

I hope you do not have the problem or that assessment of it, for it is imperative that you have friends and, as children say, "a best friend."

Janie says don't worry about what would or will happen *if....* "Just go ahead and be yourself, and if the chemistry is right and you become close friends, no explanation is necessary to her, to you or to others."

Out of his observations and experiences, William Hulme reminds ministers and their wives to consider in choosing friends that:

1. Other ministers and their wives offer the best potential for these friendships, largely because of common education, vocation and concerns.
2. Since the minister is a professional person, he and his wife have potential friends in other professional people.
3. Often neighbors are the most logical lay friends.
4. —and God never meant himself to be a substitute for people.

The wife of a retired pastor said to me, "Oh, how I wished for close friends when I was a pastor's wife!"

"Sometimes," said Janet, "we all need a shoulder to cry on, one that's not our husband's. And I especially appreciate my friends outside the church at times like that; I can cry *about* the church without crying *in* the church." Joseph Addison said it well: "Friendship doubles our joys and divides our grief." Without friends, you really cannot be your best self, you cannot reach your social potential.

We do not become interesting by accident. Floyd and Harriett Thatcher studied and observed the lifestyles of several couples and divorced people and reached the conclusion that it takes a deliberate decision to expand interests and horizons. "In the process, we move toward becoming more interesting to ourselves and others because of our growing awareness of increasing depth and richness at the core of our lives."[10]

Sometimes we don't get around to being interesting—or kind, gentle, patient, peaceful and joyful—because we are so busy being drab, unkind, impatient, fussy and woeful. Sometimes we're not interesting to others because we're not interesting to ourselves.

I sat spellbound one Sunday afternoon as I listened to my mother's friend Lorraine innocently reveal the excitement and intrigue of her life. Lorraine, who is in her nineties, and another friend were visiting my mother. I'll admit that I asked a number of leading questions which had Lorraine carrying the load of the conversation...yet I wanted to hear it all.

When she and her husband were young, he gave up his pastorate to go and teach Religious Education at a school for boys. "We prayed about it a great deal and though we didn't know *why*, we knew we *should* make the move. I think *I* know why, though my husband died without knowing." It wasn't long after they moved to the boys' school that her husband died. She, with her young son, was asked to stay on as a member of the faculty. Then she became dean of the secondary school, a job she kept until she retired. Even though the story thus far is rare for a widow of so many years ago, the dreamy part came later.

When she retired, the school gave her an apartment right on the school grounds "where I could watch all my boys coming and going and moving about and even visit with them." Then they built new buildings and "I was so excited about moving to the new campus I could hardly wait. They asked me where I would like my new apartment located and I said as close as possible to the dining hall and the infirmary! And you won't believe where they located me: right between them! I eat breakfast every morning at 7:00 with the first dining group. I tutor seniors during the day. And if I ever have to go to the infirmary, I won't have far to go."

Then I asked, "You said you know now why God led you there, even though your husband didn't. Why?"

"Because the Lord knew I had to have something to do; he was taking care of me in my old age."

No doubt, this woman is interesting to herself and, as a result, she is interesting to others.

By reaching out we look at the world differently—or by looking at the world differently, we reach out. When my sister Vivian was a child fascinated with the world of movie stars, she had a burning desire to grow up and be a missionary to Hollywood. It's Hollywood's loss that she didn't follow her dream.

And when we lose ourselves in somebody else's world, ours looks better. We want to share it, we know we can entertain without having a six-course meal, we know conversation does not require a pretentious setting.

> Enlarge the limits of your home,
>   spread wide the curtains of your tent;
> let out its ropes to the full
>   and drive the pegs home!

—Isaiah 54:2, NEB

Your best self is your true self, the real you, the one God planned that you should build on.

Our daughter Dana was three years old and dressed up in her pretty blue dress, ready to go to a birthday party. There she stood, my adorable, snaggle-toothed, pigeon-toed, straight-haired, cross-eyed child bubbling with excitement! The package I handed her to take to the party was tied in criss-cross fashion with a pink bow in the middle. She looked at it, caressed it, and said, "Oh, it's so beautiful! And it's cross-eyed, just like me!"

That's what we've been trying to say—you are beautiful, but you have to know it. Or, as Anne Morrow Lindbergh put it, "When we start at the center of ourselves, we discover something worthwhile...we find again the joy in the now, some of the peace in the here, some of the love in me and thee which go to make up the kingdom of heaven on earth."[11]

So drive the pegs home!

NOTES

1. Betty Leeman, "Lester Lanin's Bands Going Strong After Five Decades," *Houston Chronicle*, Jan. 13, 1982.
2. Ruth Senter, *So You're the Preacher's Wife* (Grand Rapids, MI: Zondervan, 1979), p. 53.
3. Martha Nelson, *This Call We Share* (Nashville: Broadman, 1977), p. 99.
4. Frances Bradsher, *The Preacher Had Ten Kids* (Wheaton, IL: Tyndale House, 1980), p. 81.
5. John Drescher, *If I Were Starting My Family Again* (Nashville: Abingdon, 1979), p. 18.
6. Bruce Larson, *There's A Lot More to Health Than Not Being Sick* (Waco, TX: Word Books, 1981), p. 85.

7. Gail Sheehy, *Pathfinders* (New York: William Morrow & Co., 1981).

8. Diane Casselberry Manuel, "Helen Hayes: Acting As Spokeswoman for Grandpersons," *Christian Science Monitor*, repr. *Houston Post*, Nov. 21, 1982.

9. Jean Reynolds Davis, *A Hat on the Hall Table* (New York: Harper and Row, 1967), p. 115.

10. Floyd and Harriett Thatcher, *Long Term Marriage* (Waco, TX: Word Books, 1980), p. 123.

11. Anne Morrow Lindbergh, *Gift from the Sea* (New York: Random House, 1955), p. 128.

The Congregation Speaks

Our pastor is so kind, loving, patient and understanding. He has to plead for people to work in Sunday School and Vacation Bible School, come to Bible Study, visitation, etc. Yet his wife will not participate in any of these. And I do mean any. She is on the roll in Sunday School, but about three Sundays out of the month, she just barely makes it to church services. Occasionally she makes it to Prayer Meeting on Wednesday night. It must be very hard for our pastor to beg people to do things when his own wife will not take part. I'm fed up with articles on how sweet a pastor's wife is."[1]

When I came across this complaint in John Drakeford's column, I was almost elated; I had read and heard so few criticisms about ministers' wives that I was afraid this would turn out to be a chapter of pure praise! And that would be unfair to you. After all, church members do have some legitimate gripes about wives of staff members, and it is important that you hear them.

During the past two years I have quizzed members of many congregations on their feelings about ministers' wives, what they like and don't like and what they want to say to you. Their answers comprise most of this chapter.

The complaints were hard to come by, really. I'd listen to words of sympathy, understanding, gratitude and approval; then I'd ask, "What do you *not* like about her?"

Very few mentioned lack of participation on the part of the pastor's wife or other ministers' wives, probably because most wives do contribute to the work of the church. Of course, in small churches, the amount of work put in by a wife, or not put in by her, is more obvious; everyone knows what everyone does and does not do. In larger churches, there are sufficient numbers of laywomen to make it unnecessary for ministers' wives to have to carry more than the normal load.

The message of the disenchanted member writing to Dr. Drakeford is one that is heard far too often in some of our churches. One member said one of her former pastors referred to his wife as the church's "first lady." "And she lived up to that title;" said my respondent, "she did nothing." Another friend said she once had a pastor's wife who was always ill; "she didn't get well for twenty-two years—until she and her husband moved away." Church members are uncomfortable with pastors who constantly have to make excuses for their wives.

Ministers' wives in Atlanta took for the theme of their state meeting the advertising slogan from their native product Coke: "the real thing." Church members would have applauded this idea, for they want you to be real. Even though they make allowances for your shyness or your frustrations, they see through your pretense, and that bothers them.

"I really played at being sanctimonious," said Janet. "Looking back, I know how obvious it was to everyone. I thought I had to *act* religious."

I asked one member about his pastor's wife and he said, "Well, right now, she's on a real ego trip, but we figure that after a few years in the business, she'll be normal like the rest of us."

"If our pastor's wife prayed for everyone and everything she says she'll pray for," said a member, "she'd do little else. Just one time I'd like to hear her respond to a problem or a need without saying, 'I'll pray about it'; she seems to consider that the culmination of any request or discussion."

I heard a few complaints that the pastor's wife doesn't take good care of her husband, which means also she doesn't take good care of "our pastor."

"When I was going through that self-righteous period," said Janet, "a member came up to me at church and asked if Tom were getting enough sleep at night, that he looked tired. When I tried to assure her that I felt he was resting sufficiently, she asked, 'Do you stay up with him at nights to see that he gets to bed early?' I thought it was really funny and could hardly wait to tell Tom about it. But that and other similar incidents since then have made me realize that one of my major responsibilities, particularly as far as the church is concerned, is to see that the pastor takes care of himself."

Other groanings I heard from members ranged from ministers' wives who gossip to those who complain (to people outside as well as inside the church) about their meager income. But mostly I heard praises:

"Every time we get a new pastor, I think I won't like this wife as much as I did the last one, but I always do."

"I don't know how she balances all her roles and still has any time left for herself."

"I'd like so much to have some private time with her, just to visit and talk, you know, but she's so busy I'd hate to take up her time. Still I really would like that, she's so fascinating."

And, if you can believe, all of this following adulation is about *one* person:

"—one of the most gracious, friendliest people I've ever met."

"Absolutely perfect for her role. She's sensitive, loving, untiring, a delightful hostess..."

"—attractive, enthusiastic, caring, warm and blessed with a vibrant personality."

"She genuinely loves people, a quality which has endeared her to the community."

"...genuine and authentic, supportive and encouraging...and real in all she does."

"A devoted Christian homemaker."![2]

What I did *not* hear pleased me: comparing one minister's wife with another minister's wife, accusing her of favoritism among members or groups, criticizing her personal appearance. If the picture I get is typical, you can relax if you're worried about members' belittling you behind your back. Certainly it goes on, but not to the extent I had expected. From what I had read and heard before I started asking questions, I was afraid I'd find the favorite pastime among church members, especially women, was verbally crucifying the minister's wife! It was one of the blessings of my research to discover that basically there is great love and respect between members and ministers' wives. In one case, it was taken a bit too far, possibly. A daughter wrote to her mother about the new pastor and his wife, "I adore our pastor's wife; she is friendly and hard-working and patient. But it must be very difficult being married to *him*."

When I began my research on the minister's wife, I heard so often the admonition to "talk with so-and-so; to my way of thinking, she's the ideal minister's wife." So I decided I'd develop a profile of The Ideal Minister's Wife. I started out with a telephone survey of thirty-five people. To those I have added, by conversation, mail and a few more phone calls, twenty-six more. Participants represented fourteen churches. All are active church members, ages twenty-one and up, and a little more than half of them women. My question to them was, "What three qualities would you most like to see in your pastor's wife?" Six answers were definite leaders:

Number One: *Supportive of Her Husband.*

This one, way and above, was the winner. As Janet came to realize, the congregation is concerned about the well-being of the pastor and his associates. They are anxious that their wives be attentive to physical and emotional needs.

"I like her to complement him."

"She should be a sounding board, a confidante, one in whom he can trust."

"She should never criticize him or make fun of him in front of others."

"If he doesn't look good on Sunday mornings—like if his suit is wrinkled or his hair looks unkempt—I figure she didn't bother to help him get ready, or even look at him before he left."

Number Two: *Concern for the Church.*

Two areas of concern were mentioned most often: the people and the program.

"It's important that she be attentive to people, but I like my pastor's wife to get excited about the programs we are pushing. If she doesn't, it's hard to get other people excited."

"I would like her to have a special sensitivity for the needs of the church and some ideas on ways to help."

One man said he was active in a church for seven years and the pastor's wife never learned his name. He felt that if she had been interested, she would have concentrated more on who he was.

Another man told of a minister's wife whom he admired a great deal. "She was a walking encyclopedia of church committees. She knew leaders and she knew what each committee did and needed to do."

Number Three: *Commitment to the Lord.*

This one means different things to different people, of course, because, as one responder explained, "that's something we can't judge." Most people *assumed* she would have a close relationship with God; otherwise, I'm sure this one would have been number one instead of number three. I found that members feel good about ministers' wives who have this inner spiritual strength. They feel that she will be better able to handle the stresses of her life and that she'll be a happier person.

"After all, this is *the* important relationship and it's what we all want for her."

"I feel more confident about her being able to help me and others if she is led by the Lord."

Number Four: *Friendliness.*

Many components of friendliness were mentioned: warmth, graciousness, openness, compatibility and "an air about her that makes her easy to know."

Number Five: *Love of People.*

It was pointed out to me that there is a difference between being friendly and having a genuine love for people. A person who loves people knows people, is alert to their needs, their reactions, their characteristics. One member equated this quality with compassion, with empathy. Another said, "A minister's wife who does not love people is in the wrong business."

Number Six: *Self-Confidence.*

Again, the idea of being real, of knowing yourself, of not feeling threatened, of having a good self-image, of liking yourself is important. It shows. A minister's wife who has self-confidence brings a measure of security to the entire congregation.

These six characteristics were the leading ones. The others, with fewer votes, fell in this order:

Involvement. Not only does she participate in the activities of the church, but she is interested in the bigger picture of how her husband can carry out these programs. She knows what's going on in the neighborhood and in the world because she is an "involved person."

Honesty. Honesty, as members explain it, covers a wide range of attributes. It means being what you appear to be, saying what you mean and meaning what you say. It means you're trustworthy, dependable. A friend said to me of our pastor's wife, "I know she's not going to talk to you about me because she doesn't talk to me about you."

Flexibility. She can roll with the punches. If things don't go her way, she shakes off the dust and starts over. She can make room and time for you in her life. She can make do with what's available.

Humor. It helps.

Attractiveness. A deacon admitted that he enjoyed looking at his pastor's wife; he also liked pointing her out to others as "our pastor's wife."

Capability. It is a real asset to the church to have an expert on the premises, whatever her talents. "And heaven help her if she isn't organized," commented one respondent.

Exemplary Character. Everyone needs a model. As a minister's wife, you will be that model to many people. It's a heavy responsibility, but it's there.

Awareness of Demand of Job. Church people feel that the minister's wife functions better if she knows ahead of time what is expected of her, and they feel sorry for her when she is trapped by not knowing.

And isn't it interesting that the last characteristic, the one mentioned by only *four* people, is...

Availability. We've all heard tales of the parsonage wife who connives and deceives in order to avoid church visitors. We hear of members who complain that the minister's wife doesn't give enough attention to her "call," that she can't be counted on even in an emergency. I didn't hear this from my contacts. Most of them felt that no more should be expected of her than of other women of the church, that her top priority should be home and her husband.

I was visiting with a long-time church member, a woman in her seventies, who had just come home from an extended hospital confinement. She obviously was missing a dear friend, her former pastor's wife. I had not mentioned that I was writing a book for ministers' wives, yet she played right into my hand. She commented that this friend now lived in another city, that her husband pastors another church. Then she said, "If she were still in town, she would have been by here with a lemon pound cake. She would have visited me in the hospital and mailed cards to me. She would have showed me in so many ways that she was concerned about me."

To be missed when you're gone—how special!

Janie and I talked at length about this, about the influence a minister's wife has on her church and its members. Since it's a fact of life that you *are* an influence, it's something you have to accept— and use. "That's one reason it's so important to pray," said Janie, "not to be the great example of a 'prayer-filled life,' but to fortify yourself for good behavior." Or as Janet said, "We need all the help we can get, and I have found my greatest resource is the closeness between Jesus and me— and this closeness can be measured by the quality of my prayer life."

Ministers' wives make a difference in other ways. My first lessons in charm, propriety and sociability were from ministers' wives—and, in those days, the only minister I knew was the pastor. From early childhood, I observed how the pastor's wife sat, how she managed to speak to and be friendly with everyone, how she behaved as a dinner guest and, of course, the kind of clothes she wore and the way she did her hair.

I talked with a young minister's wife who confessed that her only pattern for hostessing had come from her pastor's wife. "I would have been all thumbs, for sure, if it hadn't been for the fact that my pastor's wife was my Sunday School teacher when I was in high school. During those years I must have gone to twenty or more parties in her home. I was intrigued with her ease of entertaining and I took mental notes."

I talked with a few members who felt that pastors' families should do more of what Janet speaks of here, more reciprocating. One member, speaking of a former pastor and wife, said, "I was so shocked when we were invited to their home; that was the first time in all my years of going to church that we had been in a pastor's home." Several ministers and their wives have started having "open house" at their homes—like on Sunday evenings after church, inviting the membership alphabetically.

Relationships are vital parts of our lives, and how you handle yours will influence others in how they handle theirs. They will pick up on your shortness with your husband and children. They can tell if your friendships are really important to you. They can read your impatience with people and your tendency to avoid confrontation. Ruth Porter mentioned all of these because, at one time or another, as a minister's wife, she has had to come to grips with them. "It's tough to be on display like this," she said, "but it has made me a better minister's wife and a more likable human being. And ministers' wives are not the only ones who influence others on how we should live together; everyone does it. It's a natural result of living."

Gina shared with me a problem that she had, that of being afraid to be seen carrying on conversations with the men of the church. "If some man came up to me and started talking to me—and usually it was about church business—I had this feeling that I was surrounded by raised eyebrows. I'd give more thought to ending the conversation and getting away than I would to what the poor man was saying. Finally I had occasion to bring this up in a meeting of ministers' wives, and you should have heard the chorus of answers: 'Listen, don't worry about it; people can tell if you initiated the conversation. They can tell if you're flirting. They know the man. You *look* ill at ease; you'd be less noticeable if you'd relax. Most people don't see you or pay any attention anyhow.' One wife said there was a man who engaged her in long discourses almost every time a church service ended, so she finally hit upon the idea of staying close to her husband at these times, hoping he'd bail her out or the man would lose interest when being observed by the pastor. It worked."

Ruth said she was hit hard once by the realization that, by her actions, she was helping people make decisions: good ones and bad ones. A talented young woman in the church had been asked to take a responsible position in the missionary organization. During the time she was deliberating on this request, it became known that Ruth also had been offered a similar job and had turned it down. This seemed to tilt the scales for the young woman and she also declined her offer. "Actually," said Ruth, "it was a time when I *couldn't* accept. But I could have handled it differently and I could have gone and talked with the young woman. I just had no idea she was looking at me in her search for an answer."

Many members have great difficulty living in the world *and* in the church. They are overcome with trying to equate worldly and spiritual matters. Naturally, they look at you and your husband to see how you handle it.

One member, a successful businessman, was most chagrined to learn that his pastor was involved in what the member described as unethical business practices, "under the table" dealings. The pastor didn't report, for tax purposes, wedding fees and travel and lodging expenses from out of the city. He "forgot" to pay debts. Yet when he filled out his income tax return, with "free" help from an accountant church member, he "invented" items to be charged off. The businessman felt that the most damaging part of all this was the influence the pastor was having in the community and "on young people who consider him a classic Christian citizen."

Your participation in political, educational and recreational activities sets a pattern. The way you share with people in their times of sorrow and how you handle your own grief influences them. Your support of your husband and family, neighbors and friends speaks volumes.

Put this way, perhaps it's a bit overwhelming; you're not sure you can manage all that influence and responsibility. But, as Ruth said, there's no way to avoid it if you're a human being, active in the world.

I found a real hunger on the part of church members to be able to *give* to their minister's wife—tangible things, yes, but more than that. They want to help you and your husband in ways that should be accessible to them but often are not.

For example, one member said that so many times she'd like to tell her pastor's wife how pretty she looks or how much she enjoyed the lesson she taught, but there's always such a line-up. (I suggested she write her a note.) Another lady was distressed when she learned that the wife of their educational director had been out of town to a relative's funeral and no one knew about it. "I know so many people who would have loved taking food by or watching the house or filling in for her at the church." One member expressed a wish that she "would stand at the door after church with the pastor so we could thank her and tell her of our love."

When you or your husband have problems, when it's easy to see that you need to bare your soul to someone, members are confused about what to do, to risk approaching you or to "play it safe" by standing back.

The Lancaster Theological Seminary conducted a study of clergy morale. From the findings, Loyde Hartley surmised that clergy families who have the most difficulty in talking about and getting help with their low morale are those "who feel inadequate to discuss their problems." This embarrassment "may stem from the general belief that 'we are called to a happy vocation!' To admit otherwise becomes a betrayal of the call to the ministry."[3]

Your members probably are not aware of all this, and they haven't conducted a study on clergy morale, but they often know when you need help and they want to be available to you. So do not be afraid to seek out a listening ear. This listening ear may be outside your church. The members with whom I talked would be pleased to know you have a neutral adviser.

"I have this dilemma," said one member, "when I give a tea or a shower, say, and I don't invite the ministers' wives because I know they're busy and I don't want to infringe upon their time—well, I want them to know and understand why I did not include them."

Another member was concerned about the money involved when ministers' wives are invited to showers and have to bring gifts. "I wish there were some way we could tell them not to bring a gift or something like that."

(Many ministers' wives have standard gifts they take to showers—and this is generally known by members—such as a book or file that includes a few of their favorite recipes, a devotional book, a craft of their making, etc.)

There are other things your congregations would like you to understand:

—that often they give sacrificially of their money to the church because they are interested in your well-being,

—that they don't *want* to disturb you by coming by your house or phoning you, but they really don't know when the best times are,

—that often they say things that you construe as showing dissatisfaction with the church or the pastor when they don't mean it that way at all,

—that they'd really like to invite you over for dinner, but they know you have very few evenings at home as it is.

Your response should be clear. If you want to be included at showers and teas and other gatherings, let it be known by word and actions. Show appreciation for gifts to the church and to you. Let them know when it would be convenient for you to receive phone calls or visitors. Ask questions if you do not understand their inferences concerning church activities and policies. Say something that will give them a clue as to whether or not you and your family are available for dinner (or lunch or brunch or breakfast)—and which days.

Something else you should know—and this message comes loud and clear from church members: *you are needed.*

You are needed to be a friend to someone who really needs a friend, someone who may have had difficulty with friendships. You are needed when people grieve, when they have decisions—big ones and little ones—to make, to give a helping hand to a wife or mother who is having a hard time. They probably won't tell you all this, unless you ask them, but over and over they shared these needs with me.

"I am active in the church today," a sixty-year-old woman told me, "because many years ago, the pastor's wife befriended me. I left home to go to college, which was not real commonplace in those days. I was very lonely, I didn't have much money and I was working *and* going to school. Eventually, it all got to me and I ended up with a severe case of flu. I had been to this church a few times with friends, but certainly not often enough that the pastor's wife would know me. But she heard about me and became a real second mother to me. She took me to her house and nursed me to health. What meals she fed me! She wrote and helped me write letters home. She spent a great deal of time just talking with me. After I was well and returned to the dorm, she called often and kept up with me. She had me out to her house so I could have privacy for studying for tests. She'd ask me the questions at the end of chapters. She had three children of her own, but she included me at a time when I was in real need, and it turned my life around."

So what are these people saying? They're saying what has been said before:

> With unflagging...spirit, serve the Lord.
> ...Keep joyful; in trouble, stand firm;
>   persist in prayer.

> Contribute to the needs of God's people,
>   and practice hospitality.
> With the joyful, be joyful, and mourn
>   with the mourners.
>   —Romans 12:11-15, NEB

But they're saying also, "We love you, we admire you, we need you, we understand, we sympathize, we're glad you came to us."

There are a few rumblers, of course, the exceptions who complain and crowd and monopolize. As in any organization or any group, you'll have your adversaries, and you'll have your bad days and your bad moments. But the message that comes to me is that people are not nearly as anxious to get their complaints delivered to you as they are their commendations. They want you to feel good about being a minister's wife.

NOTES

1. John W. Drakeford, "Dear John" column, *Baptist Standard*, Aug. 5, 1981, p. 7.
2. Denise George, "First Lady," *Western Recorder*, Feb. 10, 1982.
3. Loyde H. Hartley, *A Study of Clergy Morale* (Lancaster, PA.: Lancaster Theological Seminary, 1980), p. 29.

The Bottom Line

A country-western song says, "I wish you coulda turned my head and left my heart alone."

You may be singing that tune. Or you did yesterday or the day before, or you will tomorrow. It would be so much easier if we could handle life with just our heads and not worry about how we feel or how others feel. The knot in the stomach and the ache in the heart wouldn't be so bad if they were just physical. But the song goes on and we have to take up our tambourine and march.

You may have observed that we haven't talked about how to fight the church, but I hope we've talked sufficiently about how to love it. We haven't talked about how to choose a staff because that isn't your responsibility. We haven't dealt with handling a divorce, but rather how to avoid it. Janet said, "We don't need a book on putting a beautiful meal on the table or how to make the children adore going to bed; we can get that from other books. What we need is something to help us deal with ourselves, with situations and how to be, ultimately, better Christians. That's the bottom line."

The fact is you are in a special role. A man in our church said, "Being a minister's wife has to be a calling." In her book *A Hat on the Hall Table,* Jean Reynolds Davis prayed, "I know, Lord: school teachers get tagged as fuddie duddies and doctors' wives have to appear philanthropic. But there's something different about this role. So help me to be loving when there is so little time for lasting relationships. Help me in my feeble way to set some kind of example. But help others to understand that although a minister's wife struggles every day to make image and reality correspond, often she fails."[1]

God knows you're going to fail, but he also knows what you *can* do. And he knows that just as Abraham was "rich because of Sarah," so your husband is rich because of you. It is no small matter being married to a man of God and being a part of the company of saints. It does thrust some special responsibilities on you. And some of those duties are to you yourself.

Even though our culture has taken to extremes the "look out for number one" and "I'm okay" philosophy, there is merit at the core of it. No one can care for you as you can; no one should be expected to. Consideration needs to be given to whatever little thing makes you feel good about yourself or helps you to function more effectively. I have what I lovingly refer to as "my Iowa coat." This is the coat I wore in college, a heavy, heavy black double-breasted camel's hair coat, the style and weight of which have no place in my present setting or climate. But three or four times a year I slip into it to go to the the mailbox or to take a walk, simply because when I wear that coat, I feel nostalgic, snug *and* warm.

Gina has the equivalent in her record collection. "Some things that go wrong around here," she says, "get delayed attention, but we keep this stereo in good working condition. My family knows that there are two or three songs that help lift me out of my doldrums, and when I need to hear them, I need to hear them!" One wife collects perfumes and colognes because "just the right one at the right time" gives her a lift. Janet finds something beautiful to read out loud: poetry, favorite Bible verses, lines from songs. And I can relate to that. The fact that I can almost quote the 40th chapter of Isaiah is no testimonial to my great prowess at memorizing scripture, but rather to my great need for Isaiah 40 through the years.

If you *know* you're going to have tension and you know you're going to have to make choices, your assignment should be clear: learn to deal with tensions and learn to make choices. Remove the tensions that can be removed—by planning ahead, organizing, cutting back or whatever is needed—and master ways to live with the others. Making decisions is difficult, and more so for some people than others. Girls seem to grow up slaves to "what ifs" and "I can'ts," and then marriage comes along and increases the selection-rejection process. We are told that in order to love, we need to *practice* love. The principle applies here also: go on and make the decision. The next time it will be easier.

You are responsible for other areas of your life: what you read, what you learn, your physical fitness, the hobbies you choose, the way you use your leisure time. Someone has said you cannot realistically say to someone, "You make me mad." Only *you* can make you mad; *you* make the choice. We must realize that in many areas of our lives we need to quit blaming and depending on other people and accept the fact that "I am responsible for *me*."

But your responsibilities do not stop with *you*, do they? Certainly you have responsibilities to your husband, possibly the first one being that you may have to go along with some things in his life that you do not like. Most likely you wish he spent fewer hours in the work of the church. But can't it be that these hours come about because of his love for God and for people, because he is caught up in a *giving* course that has no end?

My husband is involved in our church's program to care for out-of-town cancer patients. Even if we tried, there is no way we could keep track of the trips he makes to the airport, the automobile pick-ups and deliveries all over town, the airline schedules and hotel reservations he juggles, the meals we share in restaurants and at home and the ones we take to hospital rooms, the books he reads to pass on to family and patient, the birthdays and holidays he remembers, the times he has waited during surgery and the times he has shared in the death watch, the evenings he has worked late at the office because his day was taken up with his people. Last summer we traveled to Alabama and South Carolina to visit patients and their families, and, after one friend died, 900 miles away, Vernon went to help his wife with the financial, legal and emotional aspects of settling his affairs. I remember the time he canvassed the city for an out-of-season cantaloupe for a hospitalized friend. It certainly isn't my prerogative or even my wish to complain when he is caught up in this great love adventure.

Accepting is one part; *doing* is the other. As I drove in to my hideaway yesterday, I passed the little country church down the road from us. The pastor's wife was out sweeping the sidewalks. Workmen are building a new addition to the church and there are chores to be done to keep things in order. At the big churches in the city, wives aren't needed for sweeping the sidewalks; they have to find other ways to help their husbands. Maybe it goes back to our Ideal Minister's Wife profile where it is suggested that your number one chore is to support your husband. However you do that, it is a needed and God-approved part of your role as the minister's wife.

The responsibility picture has still another dimension: the congregation. They are not there by accident; they are the flock created, chosen and worthy of being nurtured. Somewhere among them you have a part. Even away from the flock, you are accountable. Carol said, "Please talk about the dos and don'ts; ask people if there are things we should do and should not do. See how other wives feel about the influence our behavior may have on our churches." Carol wouldn't expect a set of rules, surely; she realizes that every wife, every minister, every church and every community is unique and that what fits one does not necessarily fit the other, that even though there are black areas and white areas in our lives, we have to deal with the gray ones also.

I once had a Sunday School teacher who had been a young minister's wife in Florida, where going swimming on Sunday was accepted procedure. But when she and her husband moved to a church in another state, they "would not have dared to go swimming on Sunday—and certainly we didn't hang a swimsuit on our clothesline on Sunday, or on Monday morning." For her it was no big sacrifice to avoid Sunday swimming; there was plenty else to do that day. And how *your* lifestyle reflects your church *is* a consideration, even though the subject in question may be bigger or even smaller than a Sunday swim.

During an interview, I asked a pastor and his wife about a wife's responsibility to the church, and they put it on a positive basis. "If you are interested in the people of the church," said the pastor, "really interested, then your husband's work is not just *his* work, the people are not just *his* people; the work and the people are yours too. No way can they be just his."

His wife added that she has found that wives who are busy and enthusiastic about the congregation and its programs have little trouble with priorities or little time for worrying about whether or not they're doing a good job.

The uppermost responsibility, of course, is to God. He depends on you. It is no accident that you, a special person, are in a special place with a special man at a special time. It may not look like a special place and it may not seem like a special time, but the blessing is there if you'll reach for it.

"I was terribly upset," said Denise, "when we moved to the second little church Frank pastored. *I* was going to be the minister of music! Not in title, of course, but in actuality. My musical education had gone just far enough to make me intolerant of off-notes and monotones and I wasn't sure I could stand building a 'choir' with untrained voices. But I took up the challenge and on some Sundays I mustered a half-way decent attitude. Frank suggested that we tape some of our 'presentations' (more for fun than anything else). Then I did a final tape on our last Sunday, two years later. I can honestly say that I have never had a bigger thrill in all my church experiences than when I listened and compared those two tapes! What was pure bedlam on that first Sunday was harmony on the last Sunday."

Our daughter Beth took floundering high school drill teams and turned them into state and national winners. She often had to contend with unorganized and untrained members, uptight band directors and uncooperative parents. She worked long hours, dashed summer plans in order to take her girls to training camps, gave up Saturdays, got sunburns, backaches and headaches. But when the team went onto the field, their beauty left her "sitting and crying."

The triumphant moments will make it all worthwhile. When discussing recently the joys of raising children, my sister and I agreed that it's not the years or the hours that bring the ecstasy, it's the moments.

If your life has you wringing your hands and biting your nails, we need to go over this again. We have to listen to stay in tune with God; we have to open our eyes if we are to see his beauty.

A young minister and his family were vacationing in the mountains of Tennessee. They took a steep path, climbed a ridge and came finally to the pinnacle of the mountain. They stood there, the father, mother and four-year-old son, looking in disbelief and breathless wonder at the beauty of the valley beneath them. Quietly the young son slipped his hand into his father's and whispered, "Daddy, aren't you going to pray?"

We have talked about stretching our emotions, learning to handle and appreciate the pros and cons. We are designed to sense and survive the extremes of both grief and joy. You are wonderfully made and you have been assured that, within this range of grief and joy, you will not be called upon to endure more than you can bear, that you have resources and a Resource for handling all of life.

When school started one fall, I was left at home with two six-weeks-old babies and our seventeen-month-old toddler, Dana. My summer helpers, twelve-year-old Beth and ten-year-old Jon, were off to school. On that first day, I answered my doorbell and there stood our neighbors Joann Kosub, a first-grader, and her mother, Mary. Mary explained: "Joann and I would like to keep Dana at our house one afternoon a week. Which afternoon would you prefer?" She didn't ask, "Is there anything we can do to help?" or say, "Call us if you need anything." She didn't bring food or flowers, but what they did for us that school year was the absolute epitome of friendship, a deed which we could never repay to them or anyone else in like manner. Every Tuesday afternoon (Beth had Girl Scouts on Tuesdays and didn't get home until 5:00; that's why we chose Tuesdays) Joann would be sitting on our front porch when Dana woke up from her nap. (Joann wouldn't ring the doorbell, for fear of waking the babies.) She would walk Dana to the Kosubs' house while Mary watched them from the kitchen window, and when Beth came home, she would go and get Dana. Only one Tuesday afternoon, when Joann was sick, did this pattern change.

When I think of reaching out, helping others, looking for needs, I think of the Kosubs and their gigantic deed of kindness.

Life takes on a healthy glow when you're in tune with God and man, especially when the man is your husband. Janet said, "Please remind the wives that when they count their blessings, they should put up there at the top the fact that their husbands are Christians, that they are men trying to live good moral, spiritual lives and that even though our husbands often miss the mark, a man who claims Jesus as Lord is a few thousand notches above the one who doesn't."

"The privilege of praying with him," answered one wife on our questionnaire when we asked, "What do you like best about being a minister's wife?" In response to the earlier question on the amount of prayer time together, we got answers ranging from "none" to "an hour a day." Yet I heard a plaintive cry in those answers. Almost every wife wished for more prayer time with her husband. Like: "not as much as I'd like," "not enough," "only by myself or with the children," "never together" and "only at times of crisis, but I wish it were more." I found a similar need for just talking together. "Talk about miracles," said one wife, "when we finally worked out a plan for prayer time together, we started *talking* to each other." Should she have been so surprised?

Prayer works other miracles. It can change your attitude. "And, wow, that's important!" said Gina. "Your attitude colors everything. When I go about my activities—including those at the church—with a chip on my shoulder, mad at the world, everything is flip-flop. I can't find my Sunday School supplies in the cabinet, the room is too cold or too hot, I can't concentrate on the sermon, and Mrs. So-and-so gets on my nerves. The next Sunday, the cabinets are in order, the room temperature is right, Frank has a great sermon and Mrs. So-and-so is delightful. It can't be that everything and everybody just happened to conform a week later; I can always look back and know it was my attitude."

You'll find, if you haven't already, that life isn't a one-way street, that bread cast upon the waters really won't come back to you void.

My father was in an out-of-town hospital for five weeks before he died. My mother spent the entire time with him, leaving at home a seventeen-year-old son and an eleven-year-old son. The people of the church fed those boys for the full five weeks, either in their own homes or with meals they took to the house and served to them. Not once did Mother have to give a thought to the care and feeding of her boys.

Janet said, "Sometimes I think we ministers' wives get this idea that we're expected to give, give, give and find all our satisfaction and all our rewards in the fact that we're cheerful givers. But a few years into the career of church work and we realize that we are repaid in double and triple measure for all we do. There is no way I, one person, could give as many hours in service as others, in large numbers, give to me. Not only that, but in every church there are a few fantastic, creative, unselfish people who seem to devote their lives to helping others. I wouldn't be able to compete with even one of them. And even though we don't give in order to receive, we can be sure we'll never get ahead; the good deeds and good gifts come in constant flow."

The gifts, especially those of time and service, can save our lives really. Often we'd find it difficult or even impossible to function if someone didn't step in and give us moral support and uphold us with love and prayers. Recently our family went through a traumatic period when my husband had to have cancer surgery. (He has since recovered and he is fine!) When it was all over, our daughter said, "Well, Momma, you always said that in times of trouble, the people of the church are the ones who see you through—and now I know it's true."

Not only do *people* come to us in times of deepest need, so does God. Never have I felt closer to the Lord than in the days when I cared for three babies, one of whom was bent on a life of no sleep. Hours of rocking, crying and praying develop a close kinship between you and the Heavenly Father.

Several months ago I spoke to a group of wives of new employees at my husband's accounting firm. Shortly after that I was in a discussion group with wives of medical students. I found that the problems of these wives are much like yours; they too consider themselves, and rightfully so, a special breed. They worry about the time their husbands spend away from home, how their husbands are expected to do everybody else's work, that they're ruining their health from long hours on the job. They get upset about troublesome relationships their husbands have at work, about designing women. They worry about money. They don't know how to handle their husbands' periods of depression or how to use the small amount of time they have together.

But I could not and cannot say to them what I can say to you. I cannot remind them that they have a special place in the fellowship of a Christian community, because their situation does not necessarily indicate that. I cannot say to them that they have a unique relationship with one called Jesus Christ or a role in the church of the Living God, for it may not be true.

But I can say all that to you. I can rejoice with you that you have a source of help they may not have, that by your very title, Minister's Wife, you do have a special place in the Christian community, a peculiar role in the church. And, finally, I can say to you, you do have a relationship with God, you are a cherished and valuable human being, one created only a little lower than the angels.

And I commend to you the words of Betty First: "Don't pity us. We're doing all right, and having a good time trying. There's fun being a preacher's child and a preacher's wife—depending, of course, on the preacher."[2]

NOTES

1. Jean Reynolds Davis, *The Hat on the Hall Table* (New York: Harper and Row, 1967), p. 48.
2. Betty First, *No Wings in the Manse* (Old Tappan, NJ: Fleming H. Revell Co., 1956), p. 159.

About the author:

YVONNE GARRETT lives in Houston, Texas, where she is a home-maker, writer and participant in church and community affairs. She edits the South Main Baptist Church paper, serves on a curriculum task force, leads Bible studies, and assists in seminars and conferences. She serves also on presidents' clubs, committees, and councils for the Union Baptist Association, Houston Baptist University, Baylor University, Southwestern Baptist Theological Seminary, and the Memorial Hospital Foundation of Houston. For twelve years she led Sunday morning classes in marriage for young adults. From those experiences she wrote *The Newlywed Handbook,* published by Word Books in 1981.

Yvonne received her B.A. degree in English from East Texas State University and her M.A. in Radio Journalism from the University of Iowa. Before she became a full-time homemaker, she worked as State News Editor for United Press and taught Radio News at Baylor University and the University of Houston.

She is married to Vernon Garrett, a retired business and hospital executive. They are parents of two daughters and three sons and have six grandchildren.